Finding Your Place

Finding Your Place
Place
The TDF® Map

David Farr and Bill Roberts

Publisher's Cataloging-in-Publication
(Provided by Quality Books, Inc.)

Farr, David Herman.
    Finding your place : the TDF map / David Farr
and Bill Roberts – 1st ed.
    p. cm.
    LCCN: 00-190369
    ISBN: 0-9700462-0-0

    1. Typology (Psychology) 2. Management –
Psychological Aspects. 3. Perception.
4. Decision making.   I. Roberts, Bill (William
Thomas) II. Title.

HF5548.8.F37 2000   158.7
               QB100-406

Printed in the United States of America
First Printing January, 2001
10 9 8 7 6 5 4

For more information, visit our web site:

www.TDFinternational.net

Contents

*This book is about knowing yourself better so you can
choose more wisely and find the settings where you
thrive. We are not all the same. There are "types" of
people and knowing your type helps you see what is central and unchanging for you in this rapidly moving
world.*

*We see our worlds in different ways and so we act dif-
ferently. We see the world through three "lenses":
T – which sees facts; D – which sees options; and
F – which sees unity.*

*We differ in the relative strengths of the three lenses, so
we see worlds that differ in their levels of facts, options,
and unity. The ease with which we learn skills rests, in
part, on these differences. These differences also explain
our comfort or discomfort in different situations.*

*The pattern of our perceptual strengths and weaknesses
yields the six TDF patterns, six perceptual types. These
six patterns or types are the heart of our model.*

DTFs see a world of options and judgments, a world of clearly defined goals, with limited context. They see a world of simple choices with simple consequences. They are drivers, battlers, and figures of authority.

Knowing yourself means knowing where to focus – and where not to focus – your efforts. This requires a good image or map. You find your best path by knowing yourself, building on your strengths, exploring your possibilities, and protecting yourself from your weaknesses.

The best tool for living and working with others is to try to see from their perspectives: trying to see the world as they see it and trying to see yourself as others see you.

Knowing yourself should help you choose more wisely the vocational, community, and spiritual settings that fit you best. We thrive in different settings, the settings that reward our strengths and do not attack our weaknesses.

Preface

We want to introduce you to a new way of understanding people based on the idea that different people see the world in different ways. We see different problems, different challenges, different opportunities, and different paths through life, and because we see differently, we act differently. We call our approach "*TDF*," for reasons you'll come to understand, and we'll use TDF to describe both how you perceive your world and how others may see the world differently. We'll show you some of the advantages and some of the disadvantages of seeing the world as you do and explain why some settings and tasks are uncomfortable for you, while others fit you perfectly. We want to give you a map to help you find the places where you can thrive.

So who are we, you ask, and why should you listen to what we have to say about people? There are many books on the shelf, so why this one? We think the answer is in our history. David Farr created TDF in his work as both an organizational-behavior consultant and a business executive to describe how he saw people acting in organizations and work life. Most personality theories have been developed outside work life and imported into it. David felt that none of these imports quite fit, so he developed TDF from his experiences and those of his clients and coworkers. David created the first version of TDF more than twenty years ago, and he has been shaping and reshaping it since. Bill Roberts brings both formal training and extensive experience in psychology to his collaboration with Farr. Since leaving university teaching for the organizational world in 1985, Bill has been collaborating with David in shaping and applying the TDF model.

We and our colleagues have worked with TDF in hundreds of settings, ranging from local churches to Fortune 500 boardrooms. We've taught TDF to more than 50,000 people, and their enthusiastic responses have been our best validation. While we've also done the science and have some impressive numbers to support our approach, these human reactions to TDF encourage us most. In a number of organizations, TDF has become the common language in which behavior is discussed, and many people have told us that TDF has made an important difference in their lives. We think there are several reasons for this.

- TDF is simple; people get it and they can use it.
- TDF helps people choose more wisely the best settings in which to work and live.
- TDF values and respects diversity; we insist that all types of people are equally worthy, and that no one type is inherently better than the others.

While TDF offers a simple, enjoyable approach to understanding people, our underlying message is very serious. We are who we are, and others are who they are, and we must respect these differences. This is realism, not idealism. You have to be yourself to succeed, and you have to understand that other people may be traveling other roads to their successes. Understanding this can help you make wiser choices.

The road to understanding our common humanity, our unity, must pass through a serious understanding of our diversity, our differences. To work together and to live together, we need to start from our individuality. The twentieth century did a miserable job of seeing that our unity must be rooted in our diversity. We can only hope the twenty-first century will do better

We've been on this road a long time, and we've had a wealth of help. Dr. Gary Jordan and Dr. Boyd Spencer have been part of the trip from the beginning and have been wonderful colleagues and friends. Gary's doctoral dissertation helped validate our basic claims, while Boyd was invaluable in building the *TDF Pattern Inventory*, our basic assessment tool for the past 15 years. Dr. Alan Brown, Bill Johnson, and Dr. Ballard Pritchett were valued colleagues in the early days of TDF. Jerry Klarsfeld and David Harris, by making TDF part of their organizational-development practices, have brought TDF to thousands of people from whom we have learned tremendous lessons. We want to thank all of these people and also the many people who have embraced TDF and have finally succeeded in encouraging us to write this book. Thank you, friends.

A note on gender and language. In writing this book, we have chosen to alternate male and female pronouns because this is the best way we know to balance the demands of gender fairness and English prose. Our choices are random and are never meant to imply that our observations about types apply more to one gender than the other. In particular, in the six chapters that give detailed discussions of each of the six TDF patterns, we have simply alternated the gender of the examples. We are not implying any gender linkages.

1

Places and Types

This book is about knowing yourself better so you can choose more wisely and find the settings where you thrive. We are not all the same. There are "types" of people and knowing your type helps you see what is central and unchanging for you in this rapidly moving world.

This is not another book about what is wrong with you and how to fix it. This is a book about the pleasures of being yourself and using your talents. This is a book about finding the places that allow you to be yourself, the places where you can find challenges rather than defeats, the places you can find success rather than failure. Perhaps you have chosen places that are not good for you or where you don't know how to be yourself. Some places, some relationships, some jobs, and even some hopes cannot work for you. An honest picture of your strengths, your possibilities, and your limits should help you recognize when you are choosing poorly. Knowing *who* you are and *where* you will flourish are simply two facets of the same problem. Knowing who you are should tell you why some settings work for you and others work against you and help you choose more wisely the work, the relationships, and the settings that fit you. You may not be lost, but you may be misplaced. We want to give you a map to help you find your place.

1

We believe in what we call "the placement theory of happiness." People are like seeds. Plant us in the right places, and with a little care we grow and flourish. Plant us in the wrong places, and no matter how hard we try, we will fail. If you're happy and thriving, you've found your place, but if you are not happy or are merely surviving, then you haven't found your place. Your first step must be to understand what you need to thrive. What you need may not be what other people need. Where you flourish may not be where other people flourish. There are places that are good for you and places that are not good for you, so we've written this book to help you find your place.

This is not fashionable language. It may ring of the old phrase, "knowing your place," which in the past was used to limit people's choices and freedom. Most of us today, however, do not lack choices. We may have too many choices. We're told, for example, that we can be anything from an astronaut to a zookeeper. Perhaps. But you will only be a happy and productive astronaut if this is fertile ground for *you*, if being an astronaut is an opportunity for you to use your best talents. Unless you are in a place that fits you, doing what you were meant to do, you won't be happy, productive, or contributing. You can do anything, you can suffer and endure anything, if you are content to survive and muddle through. But if you seek more, you need to accept that not every road is your road. You can travel any road, if you are willing to suffer enough, but only a few roads will lead you to be your best.

The choices can be confusing. There are many roads because there are many people, and people are different. We thrive in different places, we respond to different opportunities, and we worry about different threats. We bring different talents and bear different vulnerabilities. We are different from one another, and this is a book about our differences. We are all equal, the Declaration of Independence tells us, because we are equally entitled to life, liberty, and the pursuit of happiness. This doesn't mean we should all pursue the same happiness or the same life. What makes you happy may not make me happy. Tom loves working the phones ten hours a day, while Mary shudders when the phone rings. Jane loves her spreadsheets while Tony can't balance his checkbook. We all know this, but we don't take it seriously. Although we are immersed in our differences, although they surround us and touch us at every moment, we act as if Mary should just get over it and Tony should just grow up.

Knowing yourself means knowing who you are not, as well as who you are. You may not be someone who can be happy on the phones or with the spreadsheets. You may not be someone who can be a successful astronaut or a successful park ranger or a successful motivational speaker. Wisdom begins with knowing the paths to turn away from, the choices to say "no" to, the right times to pull back. One of the greatest freedoms knowing yourself brings is the freedom not to be who you are not.

Too often, when we see someone else succeed, we think we can follow in their path. What one person can do, we wrongly think, any other person can also do. You watch one person walking a road successfully, as an auditor or musician or sales representative, so you believe you could imitate her and walk that road and you too will succeed. That road, however, is hers and may not be yours. Strangely, we follow other people's roads even while those roads lead us only to misery. We plug away as auditors, musicians, or sales reps, dreading our lives but telling ourselves that we are getting somewhere. We ignore the evidence of our hearts. We ignore the evidence of our eyes and ears.

We fail to appreciate our diversity. I am not you, and you are not me. We need to be wiser about ourselves than this. We need to be wiser about others. Treating people identically is not a mark of respect, because people are not interchangeable parts. Treating people in ways that fit them, ways that recognize their uniqueness and differences, is the only true respect. Treating ourselves with the same respect is the only way to find and develop our talents, to guard against our vulnerabilities, and to be ourselves. Seeing the depths of our differences allows us to see ourselves and others realistically. Differences are real, and seeing our differences allows us to find our way through the world more successfully. There is no other way. So let's talk about our differences.

Imagine that you need to master a new software package for your job – let's say a new word processor. Your local computer expert has installed the software on your network and on your screen the program waits to serve you. If only you knew how. You stare at the screen for a moment, but then what happens? Perhaps you'll reach for the manual that the expert thoughtfully left, tear off the shrink-wrap, and begin reading. Or perhaps you'll start the program and bull your way through, using the on-line help when you're stuck, but mostly just pushing keys and seeing what happens. Or maybe you'll call a friend and ask for help or sign up for one of your company's training courses.

You have choices, different ways to respond to this situation, and your choice depends in part on the resources available to you – how much time you have, how well-written the manual is, the availability of experts, the importance of this software to your tasks, and so on. But you probably also recognize one of these approaches as the one you are most likely to try.

"That," you say, "is the type of person I am." And that is the heart of this book: there are different types of people.

Type theories are an ancient tradition in our quest to understand ourselves and others. Twenty-three hundred years ago, Hippocrates divided people into four types based on four "humors" or biological fluids. Biochemical determinism is not new in the late-twentieth century. People with a dominance of blood were "sanguine," those with a dominance of black bile were "melancholy," those with a dominance of yellow bile were "choleric," and those with a dominance of phlegm were "phlegmatic."

These words survive in our vocabularies, although perhaps you didn't realize that when you call your couch-potato son "phlegmatic" that you're implying that he has an excess of phlegm. Hippocrates is the beginning of a long and honored tradition from many cultures for trying to understand our differences. We could list many examples, but the point is that "typing" is a universal human practice.

Type theories appeal to something in us. Part of this appeal is simplicity. Type theories interpret the vast complexities of behavior with a few phrases. We call Hamlet the "melancholy Dane" and feel that we have understood and communicated something of that complex character. We use words like "introvert" or "self-starter" or "entrepreneur" or "depressive" or "flirt" because we feel they capture something. With one word, we can say something important about someone. Our simple words summarize a complex reality, but we also want them to explain and predict: he ran because he is a coward and she will stand fast because she is brave.

Simplicity is both a strength and a weakness of type theories. Type theories can oversimplify and stereotype, blinding us to the complexities of ourselves and especially of others. Four types or six types or sixteen types are not going to capture the full range of the actions and possibilities of six billion people. Hamlet is not just melancholy; he is also impulsive, reflective, silly, cruel, and much more. Introverts can enjoy parties, and flirts can be serious and responsible. Even your phlegmatic son shows strange and unpredictable bursts of energy, humor, and sensitivity. Cowards sometimes stand fast while brave folk sometimes run. Human action is much more difficult to forecast than the weather, and we still don't do so well with the weather. Simplicity is powerful, but we must use it wisely, understanding its limitations.

The great virtue of the best type theories is not sticking a few labels on people. The great virtue of type theories is insisting

that we have a center, a base, a home. How you approach something like learning a new piece of software varies, but you have a
preferred starting point, a way that is *typical* of you. You move
out from that base with some freedom, and much of your development and growth is learning to vary your actions, to move
further from home when needed, but you still have a sense of
home. You know that you do some actions because you must,
because your setting or place pushes you toward that action.
Others actions reflect who you are, your heart and your soul.
You are more than a label, but you have a center.

This sense of home is the best feature of type theories. Type
theories claim that there is something unchanging within us –
"that's the type of person I am." We have a core and a center, a
home base within ourselves. Most type theories, like Hippocrates, suggest some biological, innate, or fixed foundation for
this stable core of our actions and behaviors. The biology that
different theories propose may be naive, but the experience is
real. We all feel there is some unchanging core at the heart of
our lives. This sense of an unchanging center is the great gift of
type theories. Much changes, but something stays the same.

We love this image of people having stable, central cores.
Especially in times of frenetic change, this core is a gift and a
blessing. Something about us does not and will not change. We
are ourselves. We may live in a world that offers unlimited options and choices, but we instinctively know that many of these
choices are not right for us. We know that they don't fit us, they
aren't who we are. We cannot be just anyone or anything. We
need to respect our limits – that which is not going to change
about us – as well as our possibilities.

This is not permission to be less than you are or less than
you must be. Sometimes we say, "That's just the type of person I
am," to excuse or justify our laziness or thoughtlessness. A good
type theory isn't in the business of offering excuses. A good type
theory is in the business of encouraging respect for human be-

ings and human differences, respect for who we are. This respect is the only possible basis for true responsibility, for finding and developing your talents and others' talents. One of the continuing themes of this book will be the importance, the desirability, and the sheer pleasure of human differences. We're glad people are different.

You are, of course, not just a type. You are a human being, sharing the experiences of all humans: fear and courage; love and laughter; passion and boredom. There are great universal truths that apply to all of us, regardless of type, regardless of background, truths of the heart and of the soul, and we all participate in these truths. You are also a unique person, with your own history and talents, dreams and responsibilities, as every person on this planet is unique. When we talk of types, we do not discount either our shared universality or our special uniqueness. We talk of types to supplement and enrich our understanding. We focus on types, but we certainly don't think you are nothing but a type. We focus on types because understanding type is useful in living our lives, not because it is the whole story.

Our work in the world of organizations has taught us that understanding these human differences helps us act more wisely. We have watched people struggle to fit where they can never fit. We have witnessed conflicts that made no sense and choices we could not understand. But we have also seen people bloom when they take on new responsibilities and people make choices that changed their lives for the better. TDF is our attempt to make sense of all this, our attempt to make a map of this strange territory. Now we want to introduce you to TDF.

2

T, D, and F:
An alphabet for perception

We differ in how we see our worlds and because of this, we act differently. We see the world through three "lenses": T — which sees facts; D — which sees options; and F — which sees unity.

Only a few minutes into Mary's presentation of the sales forecasts for the next year, Terry began to fidget. He flipped through his copy of her presentation until he found some numbers that interested him. Then he interrupted. "This is all very interesting," he said, "all your charts and graphs, but I think we ought to be talking about some of our problems. Looks like our ALN product line is beginning to go sour. Is that right, and what can we do about it?"

Mary paused, clearly annoyed, and said, "Terry, we'll get there. Let's take this step by step, however, so we all have a firm foundation for our discussions."

"What foundation?" Terry shot back. "Either the line is selling or the line is not selling."

Now Mark spoke up. "Come on, guys. We all want the same things here, so let's try to help each other, not fight each other."

"Thank you, Mark," said Mary, "but I don't need your help. Perhaps if Terry would sit still and listen to the numbers once a year, his numbers would look better."

* * * * *

And yet another meeting deteriorates. We've all been there as we irritate one another, misunderstand one another, and talk past one another. David created TDF because he needed better ways to deal with these situations. He was working as an organizational-development consultant and then as a senior executive in a large corporation, and organizations, we have all learned, are extraordinary places to observe the varieties of human behavior. They're almost like zoos. Organizations bring together people of varied skills and interests to achieve common goals, and this is no easy trick.

Over time, reflecting on what he saw, David realized that people like Terry, Mary, and Mark see the world in different ways. They think they are seeing the same world, but they are not. David found that he could work better with people by focusing on how they see their worlds. We act differently because we see differently. Certainly we differ in many ways – in our physical, intellectual, and artistic talents, our personal histories, and our emotional make-ups, for example – but David focused on our perceptual differences.

Seeing these differences takes an effort of the imagination. We live in our own perceptions as a fish lives in water. We take our perceptions for granted and we assume that our perceptions simply *are* reality. How could it be otherwise? It takes a leap to imagine that my world may not look like your world and that my world is not the only possible world. Seeing through someone else's eyes – standing in their shoes – takes both imagination and courage.

We assume that our eyes and ears are like cameras and tape recorders, recording what is out there, relaying a simple transcript of reality. The truth is more complex. The eye is not a camera and the ear is not a tape recorder. Our senses emphasize some features of the world and slide over others. We sample reality in much the way we sample a buffet dinner, skipping some dishes and piling on larger amounts of others. Have you ever noticed at a noisy party that when someone across the room mentions your name, you will hear it, though you hear nothing else about the conversation? Our name jumps out at us. People using our names might be saying things we want to hear. We don't simply record: we select and magnify the parts of the world that matter most to us, and we ignore and slide over other parts. Have you ever noticed that when you are dieting there suddenly seem to be fast food restaurants on every corner and food on every desk? Hunger makes us more sensitive to food-related signals. This is one reason dieting is difficult: as you become hungrier, food becomes a larger part of your world, and you see more food. Our interests and our needs shape what we see and hear. We select – unconsciously and automatically – the parts of the world we see and hear.

We live in the same world, but because we see and hear it differently, we respond to it differently. The world is complex. While you perceive one face of the world, others may see other faces. Just as you and a friend can end up with completely different dinners served from the same buffet, each of us samples different parts of reality, pieces to which we are most sensitive and most responsive. We have different sensitivities and biases, and our sensitivities create for each of us a characteristic *style* of perceiving. How you typically perceive the world is at the heart of who you are, because how you see shapes how you act. What seems obvious to you may not be obvious to everyone else. This may be confusing, irritating, or amusing, depending on the stakes, but it always seems surprising. What could they be thinking about? How could they miss such obvious realities? Doesn't this sound like the meeting we described to begin this chapter? Doesn't this sound like every meeting you've ever sat in?

Let's look at an example to give you a feeling for what we mean. Look at the picture on the right. If you've ever taken a basic psychology course, you've probably seen this well-known picture. What do you see? You see a woman, but how old is she? Is she a young woman or an old woman? The picture can be seen as either; both a young woman and an old woman are present. The old woman is in profile, while the young woman faces away from us. The young woman's necklace is the old woman's mouth. The young woman's cheek line and jaw are the old woman's nose. The young woman's left ear is the old woman's left eye. And so on. Can you see both?

This picture may give you a sense of how it's possible to see the same thing in different ways, and how this can lead to different actions. If you're selling cars, for example, you may try to sell a different car to this woman if you see her as young than you would if you see her as old. Our perceptions shape many of our actions.

Our perceptions also shape our interactions. Notice how our differences can create conflicts. Too much of our lives seems to be a fight over whether this is really a young woman or an old woman. This may be a senseless thing to fight about, but it duplicates many of our conflicts. There are many things in life worth fighting about, but this is not one of them. Is this like our

fight between Terry and Mary? Are they fighting about substance or about perceptions?

Fighting about perceptions is treacherous. The only way to
settle these conflicts is to impose one person's perceptions on the
other, to coerce someone into saying that he sees something he
does not see, that he sees an old woman when he really sees a
young woman. This is an abuse of power. Even worse, if everyone
else seems to see an old woman where you see a young woman,
you may begin to distrust your own perceptions and wonder if
you're crazy. You are not crazy. You are simply seeing things differently and this different way of seeing is just as "realistic" and
valid as seeing only an old woman. Notice how much room for
abuse and doubt our differences create. The stakes here are high.

Why are there different ways of perceiving? The only answer we know is that the world is a good deal larger and more
complex than we are. We are simple creatures who cannot absorb
everything that surrounds us, so we select and we sample. My
perceptions are one sample of the world; your perceptions are
another sample. You already know this. Some people see the forest; others see the trees. Some people see with a sharp focus; others see rich patterns of connection. Some people see with elegant
simplicity; others see elaborate details. Some people are sensitive
to nuances; others are attentive to facts. We're vaguely aware of
these differences, but we ignore them. We act as if everyone sees
the world as we do, but this is a great mistake. People are won-
derfully and annoyingly diverse.

This is where David started. He recognized that people sit in
meetings and act as if they are discussing totally different realities, and he decided to take this seriously. The result is TDF.
TDF is simple. David suggested that these differences among
people could be captured with three building blocks:

- *Perceptual Lenses* – we all experience our worlds through
  three different perceptual lenses, which David called T,

D, and F, and each of these lenses focuses on a different type of experience, a different sample of reality;

- *Perceptual Variation* – the strengths of these three perceptual lenses differ in each person, so that different aspects of reality are more or less sharply focused; and

- *Perceptual Patterns* – these patterns of variation allow us to describe six types of people – the six TDF Patterns – who see the world in distinctive ways.

So let's use these building blocks to build a picture of who you are. We'll start with the perceptual lenses and move on to discuss perceptual variations and patterns in the next couple of chapters.

Perceptual lenses: T, D, and F

We can make sense of our perceptual differences by using just three letters – T, D, and F – to describe three different ways of experiencing, seeing, and sampling the world. We'll call these different ways of experiencing the three *perceptual lenses*. Each lens brings a different aspect of reality into focus. Each lens gives us a clear image of one part of the world. We all use these three lenses: they are our common property, and they are the building blocks for understanding this strange territory of human differences.

So let's build this three-letter alphabet. Our tools are three: T, which we derived from the work "thinking;" D, which we derived from "deciding;" and F, which we derived from "feeling." After twenty years of working with this model, we've come to prefer the letters rather than the words, because we mean something narrower and tighter than these words. The words carry complexities, connotations, shadows, and histories that may confuse you more than they help you. As we talk about each of these three lenses, our three letters, try to get a sense of what it is like when you use that lens. Once you capture the experience, the concepts are simple, and everything else will fall into place.

The T Lens

First, we'll describe T. T is the perceptual lens that sees reality as a collection of small, concrete, specific pieces, as facts and logic. T sees the complexity of reality as many pieces or bits of information, pieces that can be labeled, arranged, rearranged, combined, stored, and retrieved. The T lens focuses on facts. These pieces can be put in order, one after another, lined up in sequence, arranged in a straight line. We call this "logic." Computer imagery seems to be inevitable around T, and this is okay as an initial image. Another human invention mirroring T is the assembly line. These images carry both the sense of the complex as a series of simple steps and also the T results of efficiency, accuracy, predictability, and order. T is like the old TV detective Joe Friday, asking for "Just the facts."

Much of the success of business in the twentieth century was the result of the scientific-management school in the early part of the century seeing work through T eyes. Frank Gilbreath, for example, started as a bricklayer and ended as the first great "efficiency expert." Gilbreath was trained to lay bricks in a fixed sequence of movements, but he saw that he could, with a small change, reduce that number of movements and lay bricks faster. This was a great T vision, a paradigm of what T sees. T is the analytic lens in the most literal sense: it breaks complexity into smaller pieces. Every action can be seen as a series of simple steps. When you perform each simple step correctly, in the correct order, you produce a successful result: the checkbook balances, a car rolls off the end of the assembly line, or the golf ball ends up nearer the hole.

Remember that T is a way of seeing the world. If you see a world that is rational, logical, and factual, you will often act rationally, logically, and factually, because these actions fit your world. You do not see the world in a T way because you are logical; you are logical because you see the world in a T way. Perception comes first. When you look through your T lens, you are seeing a world where it is natural to count, natural to create step-by-step blueprints, natural to create filing systems. In a business setting, seeing through T creates scientific management. T sees simple facts arranged in a logical order. T, simply, sees a world in which

- a rose is a rose is a rose,
- first A, then B, then C,
- if A, then B, and
- $2 + 2 = 4$.

The D lens

A very different way of seeing the world is to see options, preferences, differences, and contrasts, rather than facts, order, and logic. When you flip through a catalogue saying, "I want this and this and this," you are seeing through your D lens. The D lens sees choices, "yes" or "no," "I want" or "I don't want." D distinguishes what's important from what's not important, separating what matters from what doesn't. D samples reality by focusing on choices, not facts. Where T sees a list of a hundred facts, D says "Facts 3 and 17 look interesting – throw the rest away." In this sense, the D world is both more focused and less detailed than the T world. D simplifies by ignoring what seems unimportant. D skims. D organizes by priority, not by sequence.

D does not *arrive* at conclusions or decisions; D *sees* conclusions and decisions. Evidence and implications come later. T takes the time to line up many pieces of information, but D grabs and goes. T sees grays in differing gradations, but D sees a world of sharp contrasts, of blacks and whites. D judges where T describes. When you are seeing through your D lens, you will naturally express yourself in opinions and prescriptions, in a persuasive language, not the descriptive language of T. Your language will emphasize and contrast rather than describe and enumerate. You will take sides. Where T provides models of scientific management, D gives the entrepreneurial spirit. D leaps.

This is not a cognitive process or a form of thinking, because D does not *make* choices or decisions. Making lists of pros and cons and assigning weights to each reason fits the T world, not the D world. D *sees* choices and decisions.

You know that you are doing D when you hear yourself issuing opinions, giving advice, ruling options out, judging a new colleague favorably at first sight, or refusing to listen to information that might tell you something you would rather not know. D sees a world in which

- A is more important than B or C;
- this is white; that is black;
- this is good; that is bad;
- I want this; I don't want that.

The F lens

Where T sees facts and order, and D sees choices and simplicity, F sees unity and wholeness. F sees relationships, nuances and implications. F sees unity: not the orderly, linear connections of T, or the sharp contrasts and opposites of D, but richly woven and finely nuanced unity, networks, and relationships. Where T sees a linear order of logic and facts, and D sees the simplicity of black and white, F revels in similarities, linkages, and harmonies. F sees the whole.

F is the most difficult lens to define, because metaphor, imagery, and narratives are the language of F, not definitions or expository prose. Examples, not definitions, are the best ways to grasp F. F is about getting a feeling for an audience or a sales prospect or an organization, not about feeling happy or sad. There may be times when you are walking through a city, and you have a strong sense of the city itself – not the street you are on or the buildings you can see, but the city itself. Or perhaps you have felt this in a forest or at a beach. This is F.

This sense can be difficult to put into words. One sign that someone is seeing through the F lens is that he will begin to wave his hands as he explains, to visually show the unity and similarity that the linear sequence of language reveals too slowly. Or she may begin telling a long, involved story to illustrate the sense that she sees so immediately. Stories, metaphors, pictures, and images express F, because these are the tools that capture unity and wholeness. Capturing this sense of unity gives a sense of context and connection, a sensitivity to ripple effects, and an awareness of the texture of tasks, relationships, ideas, organizations, and operations. F seems a seamless whole. F sees a world in which:

- A is like B in many ways;
- A reminds me of C and M;
- "A" has a long history, beginning with the Phoenician alphabet;
- A is just the beginning.

So these are our three lenses, our three ways of perceiving the world. This table summarizes what we've said about these lenses:

The T lens	The D lens	The F lens
Facts	Options	Unity
Data	Judgments	Connections
Order	Priorities	Context
Logic	Contrasts	"The big picture"
Analytic	Black/White	Complexity
Steps	Opinions	Images
Descriptions	Persuasion	Stories

Some examples

Let's do a couple of examples to display the differences in these three lenses of perception. When in doubt, talk about the weather, so let's contrast three ways of looking at the weather:

- "It's 40° Fahrenheit, with 40% humidity, wind out of the southeast at 12 miles per hour."

- "I hate this weather. It's cold, it's damp, and I'm moving to San Diego."

- "Hey, today reminds me of that day we spent in San Francisco a couple of years ago. Do you remember that? It was the day that you and I and Mary went to the ball game at Candlestick – although that ball park is gone now, isn't it? It would be fun to go to a game at the new park, wouldn't it? Anyway, the weather may have been miserable, but what a good time we had that day."

This is silly because we have simplified and exaggerated, but we hope you see the point. Can you see that the first example is a T example, factual and descriptive, while the second example is D, opinionated and seeing choices, and the third example is F, seeing linkages, connections, and similarities? These are three different ways of perceiving the same event.

Let's look at another example. Consider the different ways you can give someone directions for finding a place. Once we were doing some training high up in the World Trade Center in New York, with a beautiful view overlooking the city, when someone from out of town asked how to get to an address in Midtown Manhattan. Three different people offered advice, each speaking from the perspective of a different perceptual lens:

- The first person said, "Okay, take the elevator down to the concourse level and go through the revolving door into the concourse. About 100 yards ahead on your right, you'll see an IRT Uptown subway station. Be sure to take the Uptown, not the Downtown. Take the #1 train to 34th Street, and then…" The instructions go on.

- A second person walked the out-of-towner over to the window, pointed and said, "See that real big building? That's the Empire State. Now, over to the right there, that one, that's where you're going."

- Finally, a third person said, "Come on, I'll take you there. We'll just get a cab. This is such a great town, and there are so many terrific things for you to see while you're here. In fact, if you have time, there's a great boat ride around Manhattan that really let's you see the whole thing."

Can you hear the voices of the T, D, and F lenses in this example? There is one task – helping someone – but it can be seen in different ways and responded to in different ways.

So we now have our first building block in place. We've identified the perceptual lenses through which we see our worlds, the lenses we are calling T, D, and F. We each use all three of these lenses. We each see a world of facts, choices, and connections. Now we're ready for the next step, the idea of perceptual variation, the idea that we differ in the strengths of these three lenses. Some of us see more strongly through T, some through D, and some through F. Some of us see a world colored most strongly by facts, some a world colored most by choices, and some a world colored most by connections.

If you look back to the story with which we began this chapter, you'll see that Mary is looking at the meeting mostly through her T lens, focusing on the facts, the numbers, and the analysis. Terry is looking mostly through his D lens, focusing on the options, the priorities, and the choices. Mark, in his brief appearance, is looking through his F lens, focusing on the unity and harmony of the meeting, the shared purposes and common goals of the participants. They are seeing this meeting through different lenses, and they are clashing because they see differently. That is where we will turn in our next chapter.

3

Three Perceptual Worlds

We differ in the relative strengths of the three, so we see worlds that differ in their levels of facts, options, and unity. The ease with which we learn skills rests, in part, on these differences. These differences also explain our comfort or discomfort in different situations.

We all experience our worlds through our three perceptual lenses, with each lens focusing on a different type of experience. This is the first principle of TDF. We've described the three lenses we use to perceive the world – the T lens seeing isolated facts, the D lens options, and the F lens unity. Now we want to look at our second principle: the idea of perceptual variation, the idea that the three lenses have different strengths in different people. You may see a world with more or fewer facts than do I. I may see a world with more or less unity than do you. In this chapter, we'll introduce the idea that you have a "big lens" that most strongly colors your experience, as well as a "small lens" that creates a relative blind spot in your sense of the world.

We see the world differently, so we act differently. How you act depends in good measure on what you see. If you are tone deaf, for example, you won't spend much time listening to music, playing music, or talking about music. You can't be a musician in a world without music. Similarly, if you couldn't taste sweetness, you wouldn't become a pastry chef. Your actions fit the world you see and hear. If you see a world strongly colored by facts, you will act differently than if you see a world of connections or options.

Acting in a perceptual world

Let's try to understand how this fits the world we are describing, the world of T, D, and F. Let's make some guesses about what someone – the mythical person from Mars – would be like if she had only one of the letters, one of the perceptual lenses. How would her world appear? How would her world shape her actions? Remember that we're playing a game. No one uses just one lens. We're exercising our imaginations. We're also pretending that perception leads directly to action, but this isn't true. Perception is one source of action, but so are habits, rewards, expectations, fears, and hopes. We'll talk more about this later, but now we're just playing a game to help you understand the three perceptual worlds.

Close your eyes for a moment and visualize an alien – who looks quite human – who can only perceive in the T way. Try this before you read on. Picture a Martian who sees the world purely in terms of facts, logic, and order. How will this Martian see the world, and how will she act? She'll see a world that is factual, rational, and orderly, so she will act in ways that are organized, analytic, efficient, and predictable. She will act in ways that fit her world: she is logical because her world is logical. Usually, we turn this around. We think that our Martian friend *makes* her world logical by thinking logically. But more realistically, we should say that this Martian's world is neat and organized, not that she is neat and organized. She simply acts to fit her world, as we all do.

Think about this image, because it suggests both strengths and weaknesses. It's a mixed picture. This logical approach is a beautiful way to build automobiles, but it doesn't make for good stories and amusing anecdotes, and it doesn't make for quick

judgments and persuasive arguments. Our friend's attention to
the factual and the logical is powerful, but she is missing large
segments of reality. The world has options and unity as well as
facts, but she will not see these. Her failure to perceive them
makes her vulnerable. What happens to her plans when the unpredictable occurs? She will find many situations uncomfortable,
because the facts she sees are not enough. She will complain that
people are acting stupidly, that people are doing useless and irrelevant things, because they are responding to things she cannot
see. Her focus on one aspect of reality blinds her to other aspects.

Now imagine an alien from a different continent on Mars.
Actually, we know that Mars doesn't have oceans, so it doesn't
have continents; stop doing T and loosen up. This Martian sees
only through D eyes, only sees options, choices, contrasts, priorities, and decisions. How do you imagine this person? What does
his world look like and how does he act in it? Again, we're asking you to imagine an impossibly simple person. Our pure-D
alien sees a world of sharp contrasts and choices. Options, not
analysis, will be the theme. See it; take it. Facts and evidence,
unity and implication have no role here. We have the old cliché,
"Often wrong but never in doubt" – a disdain for the complexity
of linkages and the analysis of facts. This can translate into either
persuasive, self-confident actions or judgmental, intolerant actions. Again, large parts of the world are simply missing from
this way of perceiving, and again this creates both strengths and
weaknesses.

Finally, let's imagine our pure-F Martian. What do you visualize? This alien sees unity and connection, so we might expect
this alien to act in ways that are harmonious, involved, interactive, subtle, and sensitive. We expect this alien to see the forest
but not the trees. This will be our storyteller, weaving stories to
show us the unity and the harmony and to connect us to the picture. Sometimes we'll be enthralled by this alien's stories, other
times, we'll roll our eyes and wish he would get to the point or

stick to the facts. Each part of the story will remind him of another story, and he'll wander happily from story to story, often forgetting where he originally intended to go. Unity is enchanting, but it is also distracting.

We act to fit the world that we see. We act on what we perceive, and our perceptions create our strengths. We act logically, we act decisively, or we act interactively because this fits our worlds. This is strength, but this same strength makes us vulnerable, because we may be so focused on facts, on options, or on unity that we miss other parts of reality.

Your big lens

You may fairly ask, "So what?" You're not a single-lens Martian. You use all three lenses – T, D, and F. You're a complicated person, not a simple Martian. Yet you probably caught glimmers of yourself in these caricatures. You don't use all three lenses equally, as you've known since you began reading our descriptions. One lens colors your perceptions most strongly. We'll call this your "big lens." If you are a big-T, for example, you live in a perceptual world that is rich in facts and logical order. If you are a big-D, you live in a world of options and judgments. If you are a big-F, you live in a unified and richly patterned world.

The idea of big lenses is an internal comparison, not a comparison with others. To call you a big-T simply means that T colors your world more than D or F. If you are a big-T, you see a world that is rich in facts, logic, and order. How well you use these perceptions is another question. You may be a big-T, but there are certainly big-Ds and big-Fs who use logic more skillfully than you do. "Big-lens" describes your perceptions, not your skills. What you see and how well you use what you see are different issues.

Still, there are family resemblances among big-Ts, among big-Ds, and among big-Fs. They act similarly because they see the world similarly. Even when they act differently, they have some sense of understanding each other, because they understand each other's worlds. Were you at a TDF workshop right now, we would send you off with members of your big-lens family and ask you to do some task. We might ask you to describe some things that are easy for you, that others compliment you on, and so on, and to write responses on newsprint for a report to the larger group. What we ask you to do doesn't really matter; how you respond does matter.

The big-T group will get right to work. They will discuss the instructions to insure that everyone is clear. Then they will handle the questions in order, discussing responses carefully, giving everyone a chance to speak, and arriving at a group consensus. Their newsprint charts will be written in black, in outline form. When they return to the larger group, a designated spokesperson will give a straightforward, factual account of their responses.

The big-Ds, on the other hand, will often be out of the room before the instructions are complete. They will plunge right in, grabbing a question or point that interests them, rather than starting with the first issue. They will be the loudest group, everyone talking simultaneously and loudly enough to be heard over the uproar. They will either finish very quickly or get into lengthy arguments about the responses. Their written product will be a series of one- or two-word bullets. When they return to the room, they will not have chosen a spokesperson, but someone will leap up and improvise around the newsprint report, filling in, elaborating, and dramatizing.

The big-Fs, finally, will probably be the last to return. They will have spent some time getting to know each other, looking for the linkages and connections, and working to build a team response to the task. When they return, they will often give group presentations, giving different people opportunities to report.

These differences, more than the contents of the reports, give reality to the abstraction of big-T, big-D, and big-F. Differences are real, and they show themselves best in *how* we perform. You and I may do the same task, but we'll do that task in different ways. Big-Ts live in a world that is factual, rational, and organized. Big-Ds live in a world that presents pressing choices and clear options. Big-Fs live in a world that is unified, interconnected, and complex. Big-Ts differ among themselves, of course, but because they are responding to similar, factual worlds, they will also share many similarities in their actions. The same is true for big-Ds and big-Fs. We are similar to people who live in perceptual worlds similar to our own.

Your small lens

Now let's look at the flip side. If one lens dominates your perceptions, it would seem to follow that one lens will be least present. And this is true. One of the three perceptual lenses is relatively weak for you, and we'll call it your small lens. Remember our Martian game? We'll play it very quickly here. In thinking of big lenses, we imagined a Martian who could only use one lens. Now we want to imagine Martians who cannot use one of the lenses. Imagine a no-T Martian, for example. This Martian would be the opposite of the pure-T Martian we looked at earlier. So if we claimed the pure-T Martian was efficient, organized, and predictable, then we need to claim that the no-T Martian is inefficient, disorganized, and unpredictable. And since we claimed the pure-D Martian was opinionated, quick, and self-confident, we'll need to say that the no-D Martian is uncertain, slow, and self-doubting. And since we said that pure-F Martians were sensitive, sociable, and talkative, we need to say that no-F Martians are insensitive, unsociable, and laconic.

But this is too simple. We've seen that your big lens creates both strengths and vulnerabilities. Big-Ts are both efficient and predictable; big-Ds are both self-confident and judgmental; and big-Fs are both sociable and distractible. In the same way, what you *don't* see can also create both strengths and vulnerabilities.

The small-T, for example – the person whose world is least colored by facts and order – will not be predictable. With a big-T, you know that if she has just said "A, B, C," then "D" is going to be next. With a small-T, you don't know that, and this lack of predictability can be appealing. This small-T will be more spontaneous and more impulsive. This is the person who doesn't know what he is going to say until he hears it himself, and there is true strength in this image. The irony is that the opposite of one strength is both a weakness and a different strength. Strength and weakness are joined at the hip; we always pay a price for our strengths.

A small-F, to take the next case, may be seen as aloof and insensitive because she doesn't respond to your smile as she hurries down the hallway. But the true story is more likely to be that she didn't notice you because she was focused on something else. Small-F is like tunnel vision: you see only what's in front of you. The strength of this is focus. A small-F is like a locomotive on the tracks: not many side-trips, but rarely lost, rarely diverted, and rarely arriving in the wrong station. Unlike big-Fs, small-Fs are difficult to distract.

Finally, the small-D may seem uncertain and indecisive, but he is also patient, thoughtful, willing to listen, tolerant of differences, and rarely makes impulsive or thoughtless mistakes. Because the choices seem less sharp, there is more gray in this world and these shadings can be a source of great strength.

It's hard to see what you don't see, and many people have trouble grasping their small lens when they first begin working with TDF. The effort, however, is important. Many small-Ts think they are as factual and objective as anyone else, while many small-Ds think they experience the same pressing choices others do, and many small-Fs think they see as many connections and as rich a context as do others. This is a bit like colorblindness. How would you know that you couldn't see the colors that others can see? You would have to be put in situations that demanded that you always see the difference between red and green, and these situations are surprisingly rare.

Your best clue to your small lens is your discomfort and distaste for certain situations. You are uncomfortable because you have trouble seeing key parts of these situations. Realizing that you don't see some things that others do see can be one of the most powerful results of TDF. It explains so much. Small-Ts feel uncomfortable in highly structured environments, because the structure feels artificial and arbitrary. Small-Ds feel uncomfortable in environments that demand rapid choices, because the choices don't seem sharp and clearly defined. Small-Fs feel uncomfortable in environments that are complex and rapidly shifting, because they can't track the linkages quickly. So small-F partygoers will find themselves standing in one place and talking to one person at a cocktail party, rather than circulating and schmoozing, small-D physicians will tend to specialize in internal medicine rather than emergency medicine, and small-T vacationers will travel without plans or reservations.

Your discomfort around your small lens, however, does not imply incompetence. A small-D, for example, typically *sees* fewer choices than a big-D, but the choices she *makes* may be of excellent quality. Think of all the input that this small-D will have sought before choosing. The quality of her choice is likely to be high. Speed may be a problem, but not quality. Think of the small-Ds you know. You trust their decisions, don't you? You assume that if they've decided something, they're probably right. You assign them high credibility. Consider, also, how stubborn they are about changing their decisions, because having made this hard-won decision, they won't change lightly. Big-Ds, interestingly, are much easier to persuade, much less stubborn. Similarly, small-Ts can work with facts and detail and small-Fs can work with unity and interactions. We pay a price, and we probably need extra time and space to work in, but we can do excellent work with our small-lenses.

Perceptions and skills

This is a good time to stress that perceptions are not the same as skills. People often want to make a false jump here. People want to say, "I'm a programmer, so I must be a big-T" or "I'm a decision-maker, so I must be a big-D," or "I'm a writer, so I must be a big-F." Programming, decision-making, and writing are skills, and skills are learned. How easily you learn a skill, how easily you change a behavior, depends on your perceptions, but with more or less effort you can learn most skills. Small-Ts learn how to program, small-Ds learn to make decisions, and small-Fs learn to touch audiences. There is a price, but isn't there always? Your perceptions shape your skills by shaping how "natural" a specific skill is for you. Analytic skills – skills requiring breaking complexity into simple pieces – typically come easier to big-Ts than to big-Ds and big-Fs. These are "natural" skills for them, and you master your natural skills more easily and more enjoyably than you master less natural skills.

Someone who predominantly sees the world through T-eyes has an advantage in mastering analytic skills – which for convenience we'll call T-skills – but a big-T has no monopoly on these skills. For example, our pure-T Martian is often stereotyped as an accountant. Be careful here. Seeing the world as factual, logical, and orderly makes many procedures and much of the logic of accountancy seem "natural" and more-or-less obvious, so learning many accountancy skills may be easier for someone who sees the world this way. Others, however, can certainly learn accountancy. The whole thing may seem less obvious and less natural, but they can master the materials and the skills, if they're willing to exert the effort. Don't assume that your accountant sees with T eyes. Don't try to judge people's perceptions simply by their skills.

Your perceptual style effects how easily you can learn certain skills and the pleasure with which you can perform these skills, but knowing your style does not guarantee anything about what skills you have learned. One of us, for example, is a small-T who used to teach statistics and has worked as a statistical consultant. There is little that is natural about statistics for a small-T, particularly in the early stages of learning when it seems like an arbitrary set of rules that can be mastered only by brute memorization. This small-T learned statistics because it was a status symbol in his graduate program, not because it was interesting, although very slowly he discovered that statistics *is* interesting. A small-T can learn to enjoy statistics as a game, but it never looks like a mirror of reality. There are advantages to seeing statistics as a game, but early on it seems artificial and irritating, and this is certainly a barrier to learning.

Our perceptions create a bias in our learning. Some skills simply seem more natural than others. Learning theorists talk about learning being prepared, unprepared, or counter-prepared. We're built to learn some things better than we're built to learn other things. Learning language is an example of prepared learning for all humans. We're built to learn language, and we accomplish this amazing task with relative ease. We're also built to learn to fear snakes more easily than to fear electrical outlets and to remember faces better than names. We also see differing natural skills among people. We call this "talent." Some people seem to learn golf quickly and naturally, while others struggle for years without success. Some people have a talent for music, so that they can learn music much more quickly and to much higher levels than others can. Others have talents for mathematics, reading other people's emotions, or seeing the bright side of life.

Our perceptual differences create these kinds of biases in our learning. Because we see the world in certain ways, we learn some things easily and some things with difficulty. This issue of talents and skills is important, and we'll return to it often, because seeing your talents and possibilities is the best use of the map we are building. You will thrive in the parts of the world where you can take best advantage of your strengths and possibilities. When you look at another person, however, you do not see her perceptions. You can only see her behavior, her skills. Our perceptions are private, but our skills are public. How you perceive the world shapes your actions, but it is not the same thing as your actions. When you assume that someone's actions directly mirror their perceptions, you are stereotyping. This is tricky ground, so be careful.

Moving from lenses to patterns

You've now learned our alphabet of three letters, the three perceptual lenses. You've learned that these letters come in different sizes: big, medium, and small. We live in different perceptual worlds because we mix the three letters differently. Many people want to stop here. They want to say, "Okay, I'm a big-F." But that's a little too simple. There's one more step left to take. Saying "I'm a big-F" is like saying you're a one-mode Martian, and we've already said you're not that simple.

The letters are an alphabet. The lenses don't work in isolation; they exist only as parts of a larger whole. We don't see in T, D, or F any more than we speak in letters. We speak in words, and we see in patterns. We always see with a mixture of all three perceptual lenses, and these mixtures or "patterns" are the important words in the TDF language. That is where we will turn next.

4

The Six Patterns of Perception

The pattern of our perceptual strengths and weaknesses
yields the six TDF patterns, six perceptual types. These
six patterns or types are the heart of our model.

You use three lenses – T, D, and F – to see different aspects
of your worlds, and your mix of the three lenses creates the characteristic *pattern* of your experiences, the perceptual world that
shapes your sense of the possibilities and the challenges before
you. Your reactions, your impulses, your motives, your style of
communicating, your style of working, and your style of interacting grows from your perceptual pattern. Perceptual patterns
are our framework for understanding people, and in this chapter
we'll describe the six different patterns. These patterns describe
six different perceptual worlds, with differing highlights and col-
orings, with varied shadings of facts, options, and unity.

Patterns are the heart of TDF, not lenses. Simplicity is a virtue, but the lenses alone are too simple. The three perceptual
lenses never work alone, never see in isolation. They always work
in a characteristic mix or pattern, dominated by the big lens and
least influenced by the small lens, and it is this mix and interaction that matters. We started by describing first the lenses and
then big-lenses and small-lenses only so that now we can finally
describe patterns.

A good metaphor for patterns is color mixture. If we think of
the lenses as primary colors, patterns are the colors that result

from mixing the lenses. Just as purple paint results from mixing blue and red paints, so the pattern *FDT* results from the perceptual mix of a big F, a middle D, and a small T. This pattern is the "color" that reflects much unity, some options, and fewer objective facts. Mixing the lenses in different ways creates the rainbow of different patterns. We never see the unmixed primary "colors" of T, D, or F; we never see the lenses in isolation, unmixed with the other lenses. We see the colors of the patterns.

Based on the relative dominance of the three lenses, we have six possible patterns, six different colors in our rainbow: TDF, TFD, FTD, FDT, DFT, and DTF. The order of the letters in each pattern name tells the whole story: *DFT* implies that D is the big lens, F the middle lens, and T the small lens, that this person sees many options and possibilities, some unity and, and fewer fixed facts. A *TFD*, on the other hand, sees a world of many facts, some unity, and fewer sharp options. Three lenses give us six possible orders, six possible colors, six possible patterns. The wheel shown here displays graphically these six possible patterns.

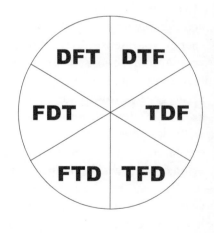

These six TDF patterns represent perceptual *types*. We talked about types in Chapter 1. Types are stable and enduring patterns of difference between people. If your are an FTD, if you see an FTD world, this says something important about you. FTDs typically act differently than DTFs because they see the world differently. Perhaps we should talk about types of worlds rather than types of people, but that gets clumsy. We'll say that you are an FTD as a shorthand way of saying that you see an FTD world. If you understand this, you'll also understand why one FTD may act differently than another FTD. They see the world in similar ways, but how they respond to what they see depends on their talents, their training, and their wisdom. We'll talk a lot about typical behaviors, but we also expect considerable variation. If we told you that TFDs are like rock and roll and FTDs are like hip hop (an absolutely arbitrary example, by the way, that you should not take seriously), that would tell you a good deal, but not whether a given FTD was Hammer or Puff Daddy. People who share a pattern are not clones any more than all rappers sound the same. On the other hand, there will be remarkable similarities among people of the same pattern, simply because seeing the world in the same way is a powerful form of kinship. Rappers don't sound the same, but knowing they are in that genre tells you a good deal about their music. You would certainly know not to wear formal wear to their concert.

We want to stress that all the patterns are equally valuable. They all see important facets of reality. There really are abundant facts, options, and unity out there, and each pattern sees a true face of the world. It's not better to be either an FTD or a DTF. Both FTDs and DTFs see the world in perfectly fine ways and can live perfectly fine lives. FTDs and DTFs will *typically* prefer different kinds of lives, different approaches to living, because they see different challenges and opportunities, but that is not a matter of better or worse, only of different. It's like the picture of the old woman/young woman that we looked at in Chapter 1. It is not wrong to see the old woman, and it is not wrong to see the young woman. There is not a right way to see that picture, and there is not a right pattern.

Again, patterns are types. Your pattern is stable and enduring. You don't flip from pattern to pattern; you don't see the world in different ways at different times. The stability and consistency of patterns is their most powerful feature. Your pattern describes your home base, your center, your core. When you understand your pattern, you will understand why some things seem easier than others, why some things feel natural, why some situations are uncomfortable and why others are exciting challenges. You will understand why some choices are better for you than others, but we are not going to claim that anything is impossible for you. Your pattern is not a pigeonhole; it is a starting point. You can do what you want, although we may question the wisdom of your choice. Your pattern is not a straightjacket. Understanding your pattern should free you to act more wisely.

So now it's time to describe these six patterns. We'll describe the patterns in detail in the next chapters, but let's start with thumbnail sketches, to help you get oriented. We'll start with quick images and build from there.

The six TDF patterns

Remember that the three-letter names of each of the six perceptual patterns define the patterns: the first letter represents the big lens and the third letter represents the small lens. A TDF sees a world with many facts and fewer connections, while an FDT sees a world with many connections but fewer facts. Now let's describe the implications of each way of seeing the world.

TDFs see a world of facts and logic, an objective world with limited unity, where A leads to B and B leads to C. Life is a series of specific, individual tasks to be mastered and accomplished by carefully analyzing, planning, and acting. TDFs see a structured and reasonable world that can be shaped by knowing the facts, the logic, the constraints, the limits, and the best approach to each specific situation. They dislike acting without plans, so they analyze before they act. Others may see this as cool, aloof, and deliberate, but TDFs simply see it as the logical response to the way the world works. TDFs find drama, emotion, and impulse distasteful and distracting. They have the same emotional reactions as others, but they don't see them as helpful. Little is gained by wallowing in emotion. The task at hand is what matters, and the point is to see things correctly and to do things correctly. They overestimate the reach of human rationality, but the great TDF talent is to discover the methods, the systems, and the techniques for making things work. TDFs are craftsmen and builders.

TFDs see a world of objective processes and systems, but a world without strong options or pressing priorities. They see an intricate world in which each fact is important, a piece of the puzzle. Life seems a subtle, complex, detailed set of problems to solve by thoughtfully penetrating the hidden order and logic of each problem. There is very little black and white in this world, so you must carefully observe the many variations of gray. You study the pieces of the puzzle, watching to see how they connect, how they link together into a solution. TFDs see the need for precision and care in working in this intricate world, so they set high standards for themselves and seek mastery and perfection in every move they make. The puzzles cannot be forced, so crises and time pressures disturb them. You cannot create understanding on a deadline. The world is what it is, and you must accept that. You cannot force things if you are to act responsibly and carefully. Their great talent is their perception and appreciation of details, facts, and complexity at the heart of problems. TFDs are observers and clarifiers.

FTDs see a world of unity and rich context, but a world without sharp options or priorities. The world of the FTD is a world unity and harmony, but the harmony demands constant attention, maintenance, and care. Harmony requires nurture. FTDs foster the growth of interactions, connections, and relationships; their central themes are community, development, and belonging. Life thrives with nurture and care, and their consideration, attention, and loyalty build cohesive groups, teams, and organizations. They distrust aggressive actions, because they see a world in which aggressive action will more likely destroy than create. They have trouble imposing discipline, making demands, or pushing themselves to the front, but their great talent is bringing the pieces together to support each other and make each other stronger. FTDs are facilitators and developers.

FDTs see a world of unity with little enduring order or objective facts, so life seems a kaleidoscopic, ever-changing pattern of connections among people, events, ideas, and things. They see this dynamic unity as personal and subjective, as constantly moving, flowing, and shifting around them. This quickly moving world rewards their gifts for quickly making and breaking relationships. FDTs respond to shadings and nuance, and they mistrust logic, rigid categories, and simple rules as insensitive to this richness. Logic may be useful, but it feels artificial beside the flow of experience. Their awareness of people' reactions – their audience sense – makes them socially adroit, but they can also feel lost and uncertain when isolated and unable to read people' reactions. FDTs learn by connecting, by participating, by being at the center of events. They tell stories and they generate images to capture the rapid flow of patterns around them. These ever-changing patterns energize them but can also overwhelm them. Sometimes, it is just too much, even for them. Their great talent is their energy and responsiveness in the turbulence of experience. FDTs are experiencers and expressers.

DFTs see a world in which options, distinctions, and priorities are strongly present, while facts and objectivity are relatively absent, so they see possibilities and opportunities, not constants or constraints. As a result, life seems an adventure, a world to explore, and an opportunity to try new things, to play with possibilities. DFTs are drawn to the unknown and the unexplored, but they handle restraints, limits, and routine poorly. When the territory grows familiar, it's time to move on. They see analysis, planning, and preparation as constraining and distracting, as brakes and controls. They would rather just get in the car and go where their sense of possibility and direction leads. Without brakes and controls, however, they sometimes crash or plummet down the wrong roads. That risk, however, is part of the fun. The great DFT talent is improvising, stepping off a cliff and figuring out what to do next on the way down. DFTs are adventurers, explorers, and entrepreneurs.

DTFs see a world of choices and priorities, but a world of limited unity, a world of sharply focused boundaries. They see the possibilities, but they also see objective facts and limits, so they see the obstacles and the barriers clearly. Life seems a battle that they are determined to win. Because they see limited unity, they see simple choices with simple consequences. They see the goals and they see the barriers, so they respond directly and straightforwardly: they go through the barrier. They focus intensely on meeting and surmounting challenges, but their focus can limit their awareness of the wider consequences of their actions, to the ripple effects of their actions. They see the world in terms of goals and progress toward these goals. They are tacticians, but they are not politicians or diplomats. The great DTF talent is to keep their eyes on the prize and to keep advancing. DTFs are drivers, battlers, and figures of authority.

What pattern am I?

What pattern fits you best? The best way we've found for people to identify their patterns is to attend a TDF workshop. Participants at a workshop always take the *TDF Pattern Inventory*, a simple but well-validated instrument for identifying pattern; they participate in individual and group exercises to clarify their choices; and they discuss the possibilities with trained TDF facilitators. In the end, of course, the decision doesn't belong to a test or a facilitator. Those are simply tools. The choice belongs to you.

You may already have a sense of which pattern best fits you. We've included three tables on the next few pages to help you.

The first table lists some personal characteristics associated with each pattern, the second lists some work characteristics, and the third describes the major communication style of each pattern. Read the descriptions and reflect on yourself. Most people seem to have no trouble seeing which patterns fit. If you are unsure, experiment. Try wearing a pattern for a while to see how it fits.

Sometimes people are surprised by the pattern that seems to fit them best. Most often, we simply have made some unwarranted assumptions about ourselves. We assume that because we can think logically or do math, we must be TDFs or TFDs, or because we are friendly and enjoy people, we must be FDTs or FTDs, or because we are ambitious and like to run things, we must be DTFs or DFTs. We make similar assumptions about other people that we'll talk about later in the book. We confuse our roles with our patterns. We think, "I'm a programmer so I must be a TFD," or "I'm in sales so I must be an FDT," or some such. Programming and selling are roles, not patterns. Any pattern can play these roles, each in its own way.

This can be both an easy fix and an exciting revelation. Just reading the descriptions, a thought begins to buzz. "Wait a minute," our systems designer will say. "I'm not really like these TFDs. I'm much more like this DFT." He'll sit back and struggle for a moment with the idea of being a small-T, but slowly the light will dawn and his jaw will drop. "Its true," he says. "I am a small-T, and that's why..." And suddenly a whole row of odd experiences click into place. When we're working with people, this is fun. Whole chunks of people's lives suddenly make sense to them. They now know why they made those choices, why they enjoy these people, and why they avoid those tasks. It seems so obvious. And it is, once you have looked carefully.

Table 1		
TDF Pattern Personal Characteristics		
DFT	**DTF**	**TDF**
adventurous	strong	rational
bold	determined	analytic
ad hoc	judgmental	inquisitive
urgent	focused	industrious
quick	assured	controlled
intense	tough	reliable
impulsive	relentless	stable
involved	demanding	systematic
stimulating	opinionated	objective
persuasive	competitive	clear
TFD	**FTD**	**FDT**
reflective	warm	intuitive
reserved	trusting	engaged
insightful	open	generous
articulate	gentle	fun-loving
diplomatic	perceptive	flexible
precise	amiable	personal
correct	soothing	spontaneous
subtle	receptive	intimate
credible	sympathetic	empathic
cautious	accepting	responsive

Table 2 TDF Pattern Work Styles		
DFT	**DTF**	**TDF**
high impact high speed in motion interventionist outspoken risk-taking inspires people engages & commits	results driven disciplined disciplinarian structured unambiguous loves and creates pressure demands clarity unintimidated	professional control manager thorough calm efficient orderly business-like organized methodical
TFD	**FTD**	**FDT**
perfectionistic cautious complex values detail measured dislikes pressure informed cooperative quietly caring	team player patient listener attentive harmonizer cooperation- builder behind-the- scenes networker developer facilitator	participative involved facilitative imaginative enjoys people opportunistic resists structure builds alliances

Table 3 TDF Pattern Communication Styles		
DFT	**DTF**	**TDF**
outspoken	forceful	logical
forthright	shoulds and oughts	controlled
slogans & mottoes	clear and simple	matter-of-fact
urgent and quick	directive	literal
large gestures	abrupt	prepared
impromptu	candid	cool
impulsive	brief	ironic
TFD	**FTD**	**FDT**
deliberate	receptive	expressive
thoughtful	relational	dramatic
indirect	nonjudgmental	open
detailed	sensitive and	metaphoric
elaborate	responsive	charming
disengaged	congenial	involving
unemphatic	gentle	performing
patient	inclusive	

Some pattern differences

When people have trouble identifying their pattern, they often find themselves stuck between adjacent patterns on the TDF wheel. They'll ask if they can be two patterns, or on the line, or halfway between. The short answer is no, you can only be one pattern. The patterns are different, and there are gaps between them that you can't cross. Bear in mind that not every word of your pattern description will fit perfectly. People with the same patterns are not clones; they are not identical. They share a way of seeing experience, but they vary in how they respond. Similarly, some of the descriptions from other patterns may fit you, but they won't be central to you. Your pattern is your home, your center. You've picked up pieces associated with other patterns along the way, but they're not the heart of who you are. TFDs enjoy an occasional adventure, and FDTs enjoy an occasional evening of silence and solitude, but they enjoy them as contrasts to their more usual and central pleasures. To help, though, let's look at some key differences between adjacent patterns.

DFT-DTF: While both DFTs and DTFs experience the world as options and priorities, DFTs are more responsive to possibilities while DTFs are more driven toward goals. DTFs drive straight ahead, toward the goal, following the plan, determined and focused, while DFTs are more reactive, responding to changing conditions, ignoring plans, improvising, trusting to their sense of direction and possibility, their strategic vision. DTFs move in straight lines, while DFTs don't. In exercising and responding to leadership, DTFs attend to lines of authority, organizational legitimacy, and the formal structure of organizations, while DFTs attend to personal power, to examples, inspiration, and informal structures. As a result, DTFs tend to act more consistently and more predictably, while DFTs tend to act more spontaneously and opportunistically. Another way to say this is that DFTs are driven by visions, their internal sense of possibility, while DTFs are driven by goals, their external markers of direction.

DTF-TDF: Perhaps the simplest difference between DTFs and TDFs is in their approach to evidence for beliefs: DTFs seek evidence to back up what they already believe, while TDFs seek evidence to arrive at beliefs. For DTFs, the conclusion comes first; for TDFs, the evidence comes first. DTFs certainly change their conclusions if the evidence won't support them, but the conclusions still came first. TDFs believe that truth is "out there" in the external world, to be found with good methods and processes. DTFs believe that truth is a matter of conviction, created by an act of will; something is true because I believe it is true until somebody shows me it is not. You can hear this difference in their languages. DTF language is moralistic, peppered with "ought" and "should." TDF language is realistic, with "is" being much more important than "should." Perhaps the simplest way to see the difference between the two is this: if you are still reading to get more information so you can decide which of these patterns fits you better, you are probably a TDF.

TDF-TFD: One way to look at the differences between these patterns is to think of TDFs as focusing on output, while TFDs focus on input. TDFs seek to *make* things factual and logical, by building, by organizing, by designing. TFDs seek to *see* how objective processes work, by studying, pondering, and understanding. TFDs organize ideas and information rather than objects and things. TDFs create products where TFDs create processes. You can see this in their actions: TDFs are straightforward and direct, while TFDs are subtle and intricate; TDFs speak matter-of-factly, where TFDs speak carefully and diplomatically. For TDFs, acting and producing matter most, while for TFDs the key events are understanding and accepting.

TFD-FTD: There are similarities between these patterns – both tend to be quiet and cautious, seeking information before speaking or acting – but the kinds of information they seek are different, and their styles of seeking also differ. TFDs are seeking factual information, while FTDs are seeking relational information, and this creates the key differences between the patterns. The best way for TFDs to learn facts is to observe from a distance, while the best way for FTDs to learn unity and relations is to become involved, so TFDs will be cool, distant, and observing, while FTDs will be warm, intimate, and involved. This is not a matter of good or bad, but a matter of how you best get the information you need. FTDs must engage people and events to make sense of them, while TFDs must watch and reflect to make sense of events.

FTD-FDT: Both of these patterns engage experience to make sense of unity and relations, but their styles are distinct. FTDs are receptive, while FDTs are expressive. FTDs listen, while FDTs talk. FTDs love to be audiences, to focus on other people, while FDTs love to have audiences, to be the focus, to be the center. As with other pattern differences, this is not a matter of good or bad, but of how best to make sense of experience. FTDs make sense of their experience by absorbing the relationships, by merging into them, by accepting them, while FDTs make sense of their experience by expressing, testing, and pushing on unity and relationships. You will see that FTDs are more reserved, while FDTs are more uninhibited, that FTDs are soothing, while FDTs are exciting.

FDT-DFT: While these patterns resemble each other in their spontaneity, flexibility, and improvisation, remember that they are seeing very different worlds. The center of the FDT world is the sense of unity and connection, while the center of the DFT world is the sense of vision and possibility. One image that may convey this difference is to think of FDTs as the actors and performers, while the DFTs are the directors and producers. An FDT connects to an audience, while a DFT creates possibilities. You can hear this difference in their language. FDTs tell stories to involve their audiences and to draw them in, while DFTs preach sermons, to tell their audiences what to do. The key pronoun for FDTs is "we," because this is the pronoun of connection, while the key pronoun for DFTs is "I," because this is the pronoun of choice – "I choose" and "my choice." DFT spontaneity is about possibilities, while FDT spontaneity is about connecting, so DFTs will typically appear more detached and more purposeful, and FDTs will appear more involved and more adaptable.

Let's summarize these distinctions in this table.

DFT			DTF
	• flexible • vision-driven • informal leader-ship	• determined • goal-driven • formal authority	
DTF	• seeks evidence to support conclusions • power of will • moralist - 'ought'	• seeks evidence to arrive at conclusions • power of method • realist - 'is'	**TDF**
TDF	• output focus • product • straightforward	• input focus • process • subtle/intricate	**TFD**
TFD	• information is • factual • observing • cool	• information is relational • involved • warm	**FTD**
FTD	• receptive • reserved • soothing	• expressive • uninhibited • exciting	**FDT**
FDT	• actor/performer • we • storyteller	• director/producer • I • preacher	**DFT**

These contrasts and distinctions are important not only so you can give yourself a "label," but also so you can begin to test if the pattern really fits. Psychologists talk about "the Barnum effect" – our tendency to believe that general and vague statements describe us well. If we told you, "You are concerned with sexual matters" or "You have not achieved all you are capable of," you might gasp and wonder how we know you so well. The trick, of course, is that these kinds of statements are true about everyone. Mind readers, astrologers, and psychologists have all benefited from this effect, named for the 19th Century showman, P.T. Barnum, who said, "There's a sucker born every minute." We hope that's not the business we're in. One size should not fit all. All six patterns should not fit you. Knowing who you are also means knowing who you are not. If you are an FTD, then you are not a DTF or an FDT. Knowing who you are not gives you the freedom to be yourself. We'll come back to this theme in later chapters.

What comes next?

Our goal in this chapter has been to give you both a quick sketch of the six patterns and some tools for helping you decide which pattern best fits you. Now let's begin to explore this map we've sketched. First, we want to talk about some of the general characteristics of patterns, to answer some of the questions people ask about the idea of perceptual patterns, questions about the origins of patterns, about gender and pattern, and about a variety of other issues. We'll do this in the next chapter. This chapter is important, so even if you choose to rush off and read more about your own pattern first, we hope you'll come back to this chapter later.

Following this discussion are six chapters, Chapters 6 through 11, each devoted to a single pattern. We want to have one place where we describe each pattern in some detail, even if this means occasionally repeating ourselves. You don't need to read these chapters in order. We assume you'll probably start with your own pattern, but we hope that you will eventually read the others as well, both to help you live and work better with different people and also to help you understand who you are not. There's a lot of information here, but we won't presume to tell you how you should approach it. After all, people are different. Not everyone reads a book in the same way. In reading these chapters, however, we want to remind you of what we said in the preface about our choices around gender language. We've chosen to alternate the genders of our examples. This implies nothing about the patterns and nothing about gender.

After we've described the patterns more carefully, we'll look at how to use these maps to find your best paths through life, how to interact more successfully with people who see the world differently, and how to choose more wisely. The true test of our model, after all, is how well you can use it. First, though, let's look at the patterns in more detail.

5

Frequently Asked Questions
About Patterns

Where do our patterns come from? Can they change?
Are there gender differences in patterns? And more.

In the last chapter, we began describing the six perceptual patterns, but there are many general questions that apply to all the patterns and not to one pattern specifically. In this chapter, we want to pull together a number of these questions that we are asked about TDF and the TDF patterns.

Can my pattern change over time?

The only answer we can give is that we have never seen it happen. Think about that for a moment, because it is a powerful claim. We have, in our collective experience with TDF, over many years with thousands of people, never seen anyone change pattern. Even more powerfully, we have never known anyone who claimed to have changed pattern. People do change their pattern identification. We've done it ourselves. We said, "Gee, at first I thought I was a TFD. That really seemed to fit. But the more I work with this and the more I understand myself, I'm beginning to see that I was wrong. I'm not a TFD. I'm really a DFT." We've said it, and we've heard it. What we never hear is "You know, I used to be an FDT, but I've gone through a lot of changes and now I'm a DTF." Awareness changes, but pattern doesn't.

People don't change pattern. Your pattern is part of your core, your unchanging center. This is not to say that people don't change. That would be nonsense. We are supposed to learn from our experience after all. When you think back ten or fifteen years, you are probably different now in many ways. At a minimum, you have probably gained some skills and lost some illusions. But you also know that for all your changes, you are still the same person. For all your changes, there are also constants, and your TDF pattern seems to be one of those constants. Pattern seems to be a fixed point within us. Through the many changes we undertake or suffer, our pattern remains.

I think I would be happier with a different pattern, so why can't I change?

Even if you could change pattern, why would you want to? There is nothing wrong with your pattern, and your pattern is not the source of any of your problems in life. You have problems because life is tough. Sometimes people think that changing pattern would end their unhappiness, but it wouldn't, even if it were possible. Taking responsibility is the only solution. Everything else is a trap. Often it seems that the grass is greener in another pattern's pasture, but you're fine where you are.

But the only people who succeed in my organization are DTFs (or TFDs or FDTs). If I don't change, I'll fail.

In specific situations, skills associated with one pattern may be highly rewarded. There's no doubt about that. There are circumstances where responding quickly to partial information, as DFTs can, is invaluable. In other circumstances, preparing and planning rigorously, as TDFs can, is irreplaceable. In yet other situations, listening patiently and learning precisely what people need, as FTDs can, is most desirable. In each of these situations, you will see people of those patterns succeeding. In different situations, different talents will be rewarded. The way for you to succeed, however, is to understand what *you* can do well and to find a setting where that is useful and valued. The way to fail is to mimic people who have talents different than yours.

You say that TDF patterns don't change, but I am very different at work than I am at home or with my friends.

Of course you are. We all act differently to fit the requirements of different situations. You speak differently with your boss, your subordinates, and your friends. You act differently at a football game than in church. You express affection differently to different people. This flexibility helps define mental health. Flexibility, however, is not the same as changing your pattern. You do not become a different person when you commute from work to home and back. If you are a TFD at work, you are also a TFD at home. You simply express your pattern differently in the two different settings. After all, you're being asked to do different things at home and at work. Don't confuse your changing responses with changing perceptions. If you are a TFD, you see many facts and few black and white distinctions wherever you are, whether at home, at work, or on the golf course. Incidentally, most of us overestimate how different we are in different situations. People who know us in both work and family situations probably don't see dramatic differences.

Are TDF patterns inborn? Couldn't they be the result of early experiences or cultural expectations?

Sure. Our important claim is that patterns don't change, and this might be the result of early learning, culture, or biology. Our sense, however, is that pattern is inborn, and this sense is consistent with the enormous and expanding body of research in psychology and biology that suggests many key human differences are biological.

Are there gender differences in TDF patterns?

No and yes.

The simple answer is "no." There are no differences worth mentioning in the distribution of TDF patterns across the genders. Women are as likely to be DFTs as men, and men are as likely to be TFDs as women, and so on. Knowing someone's pattern tells you nothing about their gender and knowing their gender tells you nothing about their pattern. Statistically, gender and pattern are independent of each other.

The more complex answer is "yes," because there are differences in how men and women *express* patterns. TDF men typically act differently than TDF women and FTD men act differently than FTD women. They see the world in the same ways, but they act differently on these perceptions. These differences, interestingly, seem to be limited to the F-aspect of experience. There don't seem to be any differences in how men and women respond to the presence or absence of T or D in their perceptions, but there are differences in how they respond to the presence or absence of F.

TDF and DTF women typically have more "connecting" *skills* than TDF and DTF men. This results from the early training that women in our culture have on the importance of connecting. This training has been documented in works such as Carol Gilligan's *In a Different Voice*, which we recommend if you're interested in this topic. Once again, we are looking at the difference between skills and perceptions. As a result of their early training, TDF and DTF women typically have better social skills than TDF and DTF men do. This is an advantage, but it is paired with a major disadvantage. TDF and DTF women, despite their skills, still don't *see* high levels of unity and connection, so they often violate our cultural norms of femininity, and they are routinely punished for this. We've found TDF helpful to many women in realizing that there is nothing wrong with their femininity; they are just TDFs or DTFs.

Similarly, FTD and FDT men are often punished for failing to act like Clint Eastwood – strong, silent, aloof, and distant. This is still our cultural norm for masculinity. Sadly, these men often respond by failing to develop their greatest talent, the ability to create connections. Our stereotypes about how we ought to act can stop us from doing what we do best.

I've taken the *TDF Pattern Inventory*, and I think the results are wrong. The *Inventory* says I'm a DFT, and I think I'm an FDT. Is this possible?

Of course, it's possible. The *TDF Pattern Inventory* is an excellent instrument, which our research has shown compares favorably in its measurement properties with the best personality inventories available. Problems, however, can arise in several ways:

- Perhaps you were tired, inattentive, or for any reason distracted while filling out the inventory. This could distort your results.

- The inventory measures *self-image*; if you have changed your perception of yourself since you filled out the inventory, the old result will no longer fit.

- Finally, no measuring device – not even a ruler – is perfect. Instruments are occasionally wrong.

Remember that the inventory is designed to be helpful; don't let it dictate to you. In the end, you are the best judge of your pattern. But before you discard the inventory results, we suggest that you consider the possibility that they may be right, just as an experiment.

What do you mean, I'm an FDT? I'm a data-center manager, and I'm both logical and well organized.

Don't stereotype yourself or your role. There are many different ways to succeed in most jobs, including data-center managing. Suggesting that you may be an FDT is not an insult, so read the descriptions with an open mind. Logic and organization are sets of skills that you may practice well. If you are an FDT, however, they are not "natural" skills. You work at them. You would find yourself jumping ahead and jumping around in discussions and activities, rather than going step by step. You would find yourself getting disorganized and then stop to straighten up. Organizing and planning would be very valuable to you, but they wouldn't be your center. Think about what you enjoy about your job and about other activities, not about what you can or can't do. That's the better clue. Where are your real strengths?

I think that I'm an FTD, but my friends say that I'm a TFD. Who's right?

We've experimented extensively with different methods of identifying patterns. We tried very hard at one time to identify patterns by peer ratings, having people who know you fill out forms to identify your pattern. These results were always unsatisfactory, simply because we couldn't get consistent ratings. Different people see us in different ways, depending on the nature of our interactions. We've found that people's self-evaluations are the most accurate and reliable ways to judge pattern. This makes sense if you think about it. Patterns describe how you perceive the world, and you are the best judge of your perceptions. Other people see your actions, not your perceptions. So our best advice is "trust yourself."

On the other hand, we would suggest that you pursue this discussion with your friends. You may learn some interesting things about how others see you. What makes them see you as a

TFD? It may be as simple as your skill with numbers, or it may be more interesting. Don't pass up an opportunity to learn something about yourself.

My best friend thinks he's a DTF, but I know he's really a TDF. How do I show him that he's wrong?

You don't. Perhaps he's right or perhaps you're right, but the choice belongs to him. People have reasons for choosing a specific pattern and for believing that a specific pattern describes them best, and we have found that it is best to honor those choices and those reasons. Perhaps you would learn something about your friend if you listened hard to his reasons for seeing himself as a DTF. Perhaps you would learn something about yourself if you thought hard about why it is important to you to change his mind. Remember that our evidence shows that people are usually better judges of their own patterns than are the people around them. Remember also that we've found that people are often offended at being told that you understand them better than they understand themselves. Respect, caution, and humility are all in order.

Can you have equal strength in two lenses? I'm a TDF but I think I do D as well as I do T.

You are confusing perceptions and skills. As a TDF, you can have the skills typically associated with DFTs and DTFs at high levels, but this does not mean that you see the world as they see it. If you are a TDF, you can only see the world as a TDF, although as you grow, you will see your TDF world more and more clearly.

Can TDF be used to place people in the jobs that are best for them?

This is a complicated one. TDF clearly has placement implications. We encourage people to discover their strengths and to find the places where they can thrive, and we are very serious about this. You should know, however, that we also forbid our client organizations from using TDF results for placement. We do this because knowing a person's pattern alone is not enough to make responsible placement decisions. People are more than three letters. We help client organizations do placement, but we use a more complex set of processes that includes information about experience, skills, and interests. Making decisions about other people is difficult and must be approached responsibly. It's never as easy as knowing a pattern.

Isn't it really skills that matter? If I can learn any skills, what difference does my pattern make?

In a nutshell, the way you see the world makes different skills more or less easy for you to learn and master. If you are an FTD, for example, your sensitivity to linkage and connection will make "connecting" skills seem pretty easy, whether with people, information, or tasks. If you are a TDF, your sensitivity to facts will make "analyzing" skills easy. If you are a DFT, your sensitivity to choices will make "rapid reacting" skills easy. Saying that these skills are "easy" means several things:

- You will learn these skills with comparatively little effort;
- You will be able to attain a higher level of proficiency in these skills; and
- You will take greater pleasure in acting on these skills.

In other words, your pattern suggests what you will be good at and what you will enjoy. This would seem to be worth knowing.

In my organization, most of the people at the top seem to be DFTs or DTFs. Why? Can't other patterns lead organizations?

We have known people of every pattern to work successfully at the top of organizations, but we've also noticed lots of DFTs and DTFs in top management. Part of the answer has to do with the nature of the organization; another part of the answer has to do with people.

First, different organizations call for different top management skills. Organizations with stable production technologies and stable markets call for managers who are technically expert and attentive to the details of the production process. Many manufacturing firms fit this description, and these organizations often have many TDFs and TFDs in top positions. Other organizations depend on continually adjusting to fit complex and shifting markets. Retailing is one example. These organizations often have many FTDs and FDTs in top positions. Organizations that are in volatile markets, where high-impact decisions must be made on incomplete information, are most likely to have many DFT and DTF executives. The volatility, rate of change, and uncertainty in today's organizations often seems to favor people who have the skills to react quickly, without detailed information, planning, or consultation.

That's part of the answer. Another part is that TFDs and FTDs often seem to find niches and dig in. They like to know everything in their domains and are uncomfortable moving into areas they don't know well. DFTs and DTFs, on the other hand, are more mobile, if only because they get bored very quickly and they prefer doing new things. This movement within the organization creates both visibility and opportunities. FDTs and TDFs occupy an intermediate position on this scale. Add to this that DFTs and DTFs are generally the most aggressive patterns, and in many organizations you will find more DFTs and DTFs in top management than you would expect because they have seized the opportunities.

This doesn't mean that the other patterns cannot run organizations. We have known CEOs and other top leaders of every possible pattern. We're pretty sure that there were Presidents of the United States of every pattern in the twentieth century. The current organizational world, however, does seem to favor DFTs and DTFs.

I've always thought I was pretty smart, but now I find out I'm a little-T. Does this mean I'm not really as smart as I thought?

How smart you are has nothing to do with your pattern. There are equal numbers of smart people and dumb people in each of the six patterns. The T-lens of perception isn't smarter than F or D. It's just different. Whether you're as smart as you think, we don't know. We do know that your pattern has nothing to do with it.

I'm a little-D and a big-D friend says this mean I'm a wimp. Does it?

Send your friend back for a refresher course, because he or she is wrong. There is all the difference in the world between caution and cowardice. Little-Ds are cautious, but they are no more cowardly than anyone else. There are heroic FTDs and cowardly DTFs and every other possibility.

We'll prove it. Years ago, we did a bunch of work with firefighters. We found that the largest number of firefighters we worked with were FTDs and TFDs. After thinking about it and talking with the firefighters, we realized that you don't want firefighters who will just rush into situations not knowing what is going on. You want people who have prepared carefully, trained and rehearsed, considered every possible scenario, and who know precisely what to do when they arrive at a fire. That is, you want people who have the T action skills of planning, preparation, and rehearsal.

Please don't oversimplify the patterns – and life – by trying to associate different moral virtues with each pattern. Don't assume that DFTs are braver, or TDFs are more responsible, or FTDs are more compassionate, or some such nonsense. All patterns show the same human spread of bravery and cowardice, responsibility and irresponsibility, compassion and cruelty. Different patterns may express virtues differently, but virtues do not "belong" to patterns. Remember the TFD firefighters we mentioned? They express their bravery by careful preparation, not by hasty impulse.

I have two friends who both say they are DTFs, but they are very different. What gives?

People of the same pattern are not clones. They are people who see the world in similar ways, but they may act quite differently on their similar perceptions. They may have very different experiences or very different values, and this will lead to different actions. One DTF may have strong artistic interests, for example, while another has strong political interests. They will end up in different environments, having different experiences, being rewarded for different actions. Of course they will look different in many ways.

They will, however, still see and approach their worlds in very similar ways, if you look past the surface differences. They will both be strongly goal-driven. They will both react quickly and strongly to partial information. They will both be opinionated. They will both be a bit distant. They will both be intensely focused. They will tend to be blunt and argumentative. These are actions that fit their sense of the world.

Knowing that someone is a DTF doesn't allow you to predict how she will act, because her actions depend on much more than just her pattern. Predicting human behavior is very difficult, and it is not the task we have set for ourselves. Knowing someone is a DTF, however, ought to help you understand her actions better. We'll be happy if we can help people better understand their own actions and those of others.

If you're putting together a project team or some similar group is there a best mix of patterns? Should you try to have people of every pattern on your team?

TDF is not a quota system. You should focus on skills, not patterns, in putting together teams and groups. The mix of skills you need depends on what you are trying to accomplish.

How is TDF related to the Myers-Briggs Type Inventory? Or the Enneagram? Or DISC? Or any other type model?

There are a number of intriguing type models around, each built around a different central core – whether perception, temperament, information processing, emotional response, or some other process. Because each is based on a different core process, they don't map onto each other with any precision. Knowing that you are a TFD doesn't allow us to predict your MBTI type or your Enneagram group. We've learned things about ourselves from each of these models, and we are certain that you can as well. Explore the different models and take what is valuable to you. Don't worry too much about trying to fit all the pieces together. The result would be so complex that it would confuse more than it would illuminate.

Aren't labels dangerous? Can't they be used to discriminate against people?

Yes, labels are dangerous. Yes, they can be used to discriminate. So be careful and thoughtful. Human beings are not going to stop using labels and categories. They are too useful. We believe the categories we are using are helpful, but we have seen them misused. When you see our language, or any language, being misused, speak up.

Some last words

- Patterns are types. They are the starting points, the core and central tendency in a person's behavior, not rigid limits or convenient excuses.
- All six patterns are equally good and valuable.
- Stereotyping is dangerous. People are bigger than labels.

6

The TDF Pattern

TDFs see a world of facts and logic, a segmented world with limited unity. They see a world that is structured and reasonable. TDFs are planners, craftsman, and builders.

Libby is a TDF who works as a sales manager for a large telemarketing operation. She arrives at work early and walks quickly past the few early-shift people on the phones, nodding as she passes. She puts her coffee on the desk of her small office and shuts the door. She sets this time aside every morning to prepare for the day. She checks her voice mail and her e-mail for emergencies and then prints out the numbers from the day before and begins to study them, making notes in the margins, and then sending quick e-mails to several of her people about their performance. She wants those messages on their machines when they arrive. She scans her calendar for the day and sees no surprises. She's working her way through her e-mail when Tom knocks on her door and comes in. She likes Tom; he's a hard worker.

"I had an e-mail to come and see you," he says. He looks upset.

"Yes, come in and have a seat," Libby replies, "and shut the door, if you would."

"I know I'm not doing very well right now," Tom says, "and I'm really sorry." He bites his lip.

"Yes, your numbers are down. I'm surprised, because you've been solid until now. What seems to be the problem?"

"I don't know," Tom replies. "I think maybe it's this new product line. I'm just not comfortable with it."

"Well," says Libby, "I've been listening to your tapes, and you are sounding very tentative. You're also deviating from script a good deal."

"I'm just not comfortable," Tom says.

Libby frowns. She looks at her calendar. "I've got half an hour at 2:30," she says, "so let's plan a side-by-side, and we'll walk through this step-by-step and see if we can't identify the problem."

Tom nods, his forehead furrowed. "I'll see you then," he says. He hesitates, and then he leaves. Libby thinks for a moment, makes a note on her calendar, and then turns back to her e-mail.

* * * * *

Libby, like all TDFs, sees a world that is rational and sensible, logical and factual. Things are what they are. She sees a functional world, where coffee makers make coffee and sales people make sales. Libby works by planning, preparing, and persevering. She sees a world of things to be done and projects to be carried out, a world of responsibilities to master and tasks to perform. She knows that all these tasks can be mastered and all these jobs can be performed. There are no mysteries to selling, for example. There is only inadequate information, inadequate analysis, and inadequate planning. Tasks like selling and coaching are not vague or fuzzy, intuitive or emotional. Only bad planning or incompetent action is vague and fuzzy, intuitive and emotional. Gut feelings, intuitions, inspirations, and raw emotions are poor substitutes for logic, preparation, and hard work.

Libby is not impressed when people talk about how complex and subtle and difficult the world is. Complexity is just unanalyzed simplicity. The most complex task can always be broken down into a sequence of simple steps. An automobile is a complex machine, but you can build it most efficiently by seeing it as Henry Ford did, as a sequence of simple steps on an assembly line. The assembly line is one image of the TDF world, but don't be misled into believing this approach only fits machines. A painting or a piece of music or a sale is also a sequence of simple steps. Negotiation, mediation, and building friendships are sequences of steps. The art lies in identifying the steps and planning the sequence.

Libby is "businesslike." We can describe her as task-oriented, logical, and orderly, but don't let this fool you into believing that Libby is "all work and no play" or that she is just another piece of office equipment. Libby, like all people, is complex and multisided. She has two sons whom she adores. She plays a fair game of tennis, enjoys silly movies, and restores old furniture. She knows how to have fun; she knows how to laugh; she knows how to waste time. She appears businesslike because her world is businesslike.

We've described TDFs in earlier chapters as rational, industrious, controlled, professional, orderly, methodical, logical, matter-of-fact, and cool, but understanding this means understanding Libby's world, a world in which logic, control, and order are the most effective responses. Libby sees a world where "cool" is more caring than "warm" and method is more powerful than passion. Her great talents are her objectivity, rationality, analysis, and planning. These talents allow Libby to act sensibly and properly in an objective and rational world. She seeks firm ground for acting – a clear understanding of the steps and sequences – so her actions will work. Libby's approach is solid, thoughtful, and deliberate, because that approach works in a factual, orderly world. She doesn't act impulsively or randomly. She doesn't flail about. She acts when she has clarified the uncertain and cleared the muddle. She observes and she plans. She takes things step by step, with each step leading forward to the next, one step at a time, until the job is done.

This is also her great weakness. Libby has trouble acting before she is clear, before she has planned carefully. She has trouble reacting quickly, on the spot, to changing circumstances. Libby does not like surprises. The unexpected, she feels, requires new thinking and new planning, not quick reactions or spontaneity. You must step back in order to see more clearly. She mistrusts the irrational, the unplanned, and the spontaneous. Passion, impulse, and intuition are parts of our common humanity, but Libby mistrusts these both in herself and in others. She has seen that when she reacts impulsively, she makes mistakes. She hesitates to change directions or act without a plan. Her friends claim that she schedules her spontaneity: "Next Thursday at 3:00 p.m., be spontaneous;" "Next Monday at 10:00 a.m., adopt a new plan."

A mature TDF like Libby, however, has learned both flexibility and tolerance. One sign of this is her humor. Her humor is ironic, recognizing that while the world should be rational and sensible, individual events are sometimes irrational and absurd. She has learned to accept and laugh at the illogical and to see her own yearning for logic as a bit illogical. She can make fun of her own desire for plans and order in a chaotic world. You can value your way of seeing things while still knowing its limits.

Perhaps the best image for Libby is the craftsman, the one who knows how to do things and cares deeply that things are done well. Libby's great talent is her sense of craft. Calm, stability, and assurance are her hallmarks, rooted in her certainty that the job can be done, that it can be sorted through, clarified, planned, and performed. She applies this to her work, to her tennis, and to her most important job as a mother. Impulse and gut reactions will only lead to poor, sloppy work. Libby works from plans in every part of her life, although this is so natural to her that she is often unaware of how much she has planned. Thought and planning are the heart of her performances. Picture the cabinetmaker studying the space, studying the wood, drawing a plan, measuring carefully, and setting to work.

Proper method and technique are central to Libby's sense of craft. There is a right way to do things, a way that fits the task, and acting any other way simply makes things harder than they need to be. Discovering the right technique, creating the right tools, is her passion. She loves to beat back the apparent chaos and confusion. Giving people the right tools, Libby has found, makes all the difference. Anyone can sell, she believes, if they're given the right tools and shown how to use them. There are proper tools for each job, and Libby loves the right tools. She doesn't use screwdrivers to open paint cans; screwdrivers drive screws and pry bars open paint cans. As a result, her screwdrivers never have bunged or bent tips.

Because she loves to build order, Libby's primary focus is not on knowledge but on skill. Libby doesn't value knowledge for its own sake, but she does value craft and skill. Her knowledge is not abstract; it is not "what" but "how." Libby trusts and respects craft as much as she mistrusts impulse, intuition, and improvisation. Libby focuses on "how" – on how to improve sales, on how to help a struggling salesperson, on how to help her children become responsible and loving adults, on how to improve her ground stroke in tennis.

One of the qualities people admire in Libby is her perseverance. She finishes what she starts. Libby's perseverance grows from her conviction that good plans produce results, if you follow the plan step by step to the end. She has found that inspiration and enthusiasm, while fun, are unreliable. In telemarketing, you have good days and bad days, but if you stick to the proper procedures, you will succeed. You succeed by following a plan, and if you have a plan, you don't need to wait for inspiration. You know what to do next. People describe her as goal-oriented, but that's not quite right. She is plan oriented. This can be a problem if the plan is wrong, but Libby has learned to stand back occasionally to check where the plan is taking her.

Libby learns by this same process of observing, planning, and persevering. She learns most comfortably when she is given access to information and left alone. She doesn't find discussion, dialogue, or debate especially helpful, and she dislikes attempts to make learning "relevant" or personal. These are useless frills for her, distractions from the task of mastering the information. Libby dislikes her company's sales training program, for example, because it focuses on motivation. Libby thinks the only motivation people need is a well-designed incentive program. All people need from training is to be shown how to do the job. They need simple step-by-step instructions to take them through the task. Libby learns by gathering and organizing information, making lists, drawing up comparisons, making outlines and flowcharts, card files and cross-indexes. She learns by acting on the information, trying to build order within it, trying to learn the rules for this information.

In the end, Libby learns rules, because knowing the rules allows her to act skillfully. Libby distinguishes sharply, for example, between work and play. These are different categories of behavior, because there are different roles to be played, different expectations, and different rules. You even wear different clothes to work and play. You cannot be both a friend and a manager at the same time, for example, and no good can come of confusing these roles. She has seen it time after time. Being a good friend follows different rules than being a good manager. After work, you can be friends or play together, because then you are in a different setting, with different rules. These kinds of rules are not arbitrary. Rules and roles are tools for behaving well, because they reflect important facts about the world. Rules and roles express the craftsman's sense of the world's logic.

The same principles also govern Libby's approach to human interactions. Her sense of craft covers her dealings with people as well as with things and information, so she observes people carefully, arranges her observations logically, plans, and then acts deliberately and skillfully on her conclusions. Libby approaches conflict, for example, as a matter for negotiation. You take an objective approach, you break the conflict down into smaller chunks, and then you deal with the smaller chunks one at a time. When an employee is upset about a performance evaluation, for example, Libby sits with him and works through the evaluation form item by item, identifying areas of disagreement, and then works with each area of disagreement, identifying concrete instances to support the differing perceptions. She focuses on the facts and obtaining agreement about the facts. When people agree on the facts, she assumes, there is nothing left to disagree about.

This belief in natural rules can make Libby seem predictable or even rigid, even to herself. She laughs at herself because she always pays her bills on the first and third Thursday evening of each month, but it works so well that she can't imagine changing. She loves finding the best way of doing things, the right way, the way that captures the logic of the world. We have found that people sometimes confuse the TDF pattern with obsessive-compulsive behavior, but the two are miles apart. Obsessive-compulsive behavior is a disorder. It is rigid and uncontrolled, inflexible and maladaptive. Obsessive-compulsive behavior hurts. Perhaps it comes from poor toilet training, as Freud thought, or perhaps it comes from a brain malfunction, as current research on drug effects suggests. Whatever its source, obsessive-compulsive behavior is pathological. Being a TDF is not pathological: none of the TDF patterns is pathological.

Watch Libby master a new sport, for example, and you will be observing a very healthy process: she observes carefully as others perform; she takes lessons; she practices over and over; and she takes more lessons, working to do these new skills properly and well. Observe and practice, observe and practice. This kind of mastery is a triumph. If Libby does sometimes become a bit rigid, that is still not a disease.

Libby expresses her creativity by making things work well, not by putting a personal or idiosyncratic stamp on her work. The idea of doing things your own way mystifies and confuses Libby. "I don't do it my way," she likes to say, "I do it the right way." Libby expresses her creativity by solving problems. Tom has a problem selling this new product line, for example, and Libby will work hard to identify and fix this problem. She can be brilliant in planning and designing, taking an idea and identifying problems, correcting inefficiencies, and making things work. She has the tenacity, the patience, and the fascination to examine, adjust, fiddle, and solve. She doesn't give up; she knows anything can be fixed. This form of creativity is widely underrated and under-appreciated. Libby will figure out why Tom's sales numbers are down, and she will help him fix the problem.

Libby handles even the most personal problems this way, focusing on what she can see and what she can do and not worrying about any underlying, deep psychological processes. Libby spends little time pondering what people *really* want or *really* think. She doesn't think about people's hidden agendas or try to read between the lines. She basically takes people at face value. She sees herself as straightforward, and she assumes everyone else is as well. She has little interest in self-analysis, although she does enjoy books and ideas that help her perform more skillfully. She's not particularly interested in *why* she does things; she just wants to do things well. She finds skill more intriguing than motives. Tom shows signs of being upset and bothered, but Libby assumes that if they fix his sales problem, that will also fix his upset. She sees psychology as simple and mechanical, mostly genetics and biology. To look inside is to look in the wrong direction, because you perform in the world, not in your head. Skill counts most.

Libby's look of mastery sometimes leads people to turn to her for quick, spot judgments, but this is a mistake. When forced to make quick assessments, Libby can be negative and critical. When Libby's boss had a new idea for how to move new employees from training onto the floor, he ran it by Libby for her reaction. What she saw first was the contrast between the sketchiness and incompleteness of the new idea and the well-tested current procedure. In this perspective, the new always suffers. The new is never as well tested as the old, whether it is a new workflow or a new menu item in a favorite restaurant. This critical bias, however, should not be taken too seriously. Libby was not saying "no." Given a few moments, her bias evaporated as she filled in the blanks and generated lengthy and fair listings of the pros and cons of both the old and the new. But it took a little time. Don't look to Libby for a quick response unless you want to hear a "no." She needs time to get to "yes."

Libby loves situations that demand thoroughness, follow through, and completion. Taking on a task, organizing it, implementing it, and bringing it to completion deeply satisfies her. Tying up the loose ends, clearing up the fuzziness, and producing a finished product shows that she has done the job correctly and validates her persistence and hard work. She dislikes situations that are chaotic, emotional, or confused, situations that resist clarifying, planning, and straightforward action. While convinced that there is a right way and a right answer in any situation, Libby knows that there is always more to learn. She welcomes new information and new perspectives for the information they bring and the help they offer. Truth may be fixed, but the search is continuous. You never fully master your craft.

Libby, of course, is just as emotional as anyone else. She feels fear, love, hate, pleasure, jealousy, sadness, and excitement, just as everyone does. She tends, however, to treat her emotions as facts to be observed, analyzed, and planned and controlled, like other facts. The result is that Libby, like most TDFs, tends to express emotions less than other people do. Libby doesn't talk much about her feelings, nor does she show her feelings strongly.

She doesn't see the point. Why should she tell people she likes them when her actions show that she does. How does yelling and screaming help when you're angry? This does not mean, however, that Libby is cold or unfeeling. People who know her well know how warm and caring she is.

To others, however, her style can make Libby seem distant, removed, stiff, and unfeeling. While TDFs seem calm, stable, and unflappable – masters of their worlds – they can also look cold, aloof, and uncaring. Libby analyzes before she acts, and this looks mechanical and cold to some people. This is unfair, but it happens. Libby has frequently been beaten-up about her "aloofness," so she is very sensitive about her skills with people. She claims she would rather be respected than popular. There is some truth to this, but it also hurts her that people seem not to understand her. She went through a period of thinking that she shouldn't be a manager because people thought she was cold and unfeeling, but she learned that this ignored the real strengths – human as well as technical – that she brings to her interactions.

Libby cares about people and enjoys being with people, but she prefers settings where she understands her role, where she can act on clear and structured expectations, where she knows what she is doing, what the rules are. She doesn't like situations where she can't plan and prepare. When she goes to a cocktail party, for example, she has in mind several appropriate topics of conversation, and she plans her circuit of the room. She brings structure to the situation. Her parties have games and dances and assigned places. Her vacations are well planned and beautifully mapped. Unstructured or poorly planned situations, new or unexpected situations, parties where one mills around with strangers, projects where expectations have to be grasped on the fly and where there are no defined roles, are much less comfortable for Libby, and she will avoid these situations if she can.

People know her value. Libby brings real strength to the groups in which she participates. She stabilizes groups. Her preparation and objectivity bring calm, and her insistence on clear expectations and roles defuses tensions. People depend on her to bring structure to their interactions. There is little need to slug it out when her objective and fair services are available. People trust her to be impartial and disinterested. They know that she doesn't get involved in political maneuvering or intrigues. These actions don't make much sense to her, but this "disability" gives her credibility and influence. Libby works well from a role "above politics." She moves debate away from the personal and political and toward concrete issues. She focuses on the tasks the group is trying to accomplish. Even in her social groups, Libby will make sure that the "work" of the group is being done: that reservations have been made, that everyone knows the plans, and that everyone has a way to get home. This is a comfortable role for her. She is content on the edges of a group, moving to the center when the task calls for it, but happy to move back to the edges afterward. From the edges, she can see better.

Sometimes, sadly, her objectivity infuriates people. People who work or live with Libby sometimes feel offended at being treated objectively or as a project, and they'll try to provoke personal reactions from her. People, oddly enough, aren't always satisfied to be treated skillfully, properly, and well. Sometimes they wish to be treated affectionately, personally, and intimately. Learning to step outside of the task with a few special people is a key growth edge for Libby.

Libby's TDF sense of craft shows also in her communication and in her language. She uses language to describe, not to embellish, not to persuade, not to connect or interact. She describes what she sees, simply, logically, and clearly. She likes to understate. She's uncomfortable with adjectives and dramatics. The facts, she thinks, will speak for themselves, so there is no point in adding opinions, judgments, reactions, or feelings. The facts are enough. This is another important growth point for her. Libby needs to understand that facts do not and cannot speak for themselves; the facts must be spoken for and their implications must be spelled out. In drawing a conclusion, making a judgment, giving a reaction, she may feel she is being obvious and trivial, but what is obvious to her is not obvious to others. She needs to conclude, to judge, and react.

When selling a product, for example, Libby feels it should be enough to spell out the features of the product. The advantages of these features should be obvious to the customer. She thinks that the advantages are too obvious to require elaboration, but this is wrong. To many people, the advantages are not obvious. TDFs are best sold to by simply describing the features of a product as carefully and accurately as possible, but they need to appreciate that people often want more. As a salesperson, Libby has learned this lesson, but she still sometimes feels silly saying things that seem so obvious.

While the TDF bias toward simple description needs to be supplemented, it should not be abandoned. Libby's influence and power grow largely from her skill and her objectivity, from her appearance of expertise. Libby sells best, she influences best, when she is seen as objective and fair, when she is seen as not selling or not persuading. People trust Libby as a "content expert," knowing that she will not misunderstand or misrepresent the facts and logic of the situation. Respect for facts and logic is the heart of Libby's integrity, and her integrity is the heart of her power and influence. The heart of TDF power is their reputation for expertise.

Her content focus is also evident in the way that Libby listens. Libby hears what people are saying, but she sometimes misses how they are saying it. She doesn't read between the lines. She doesn't read the subtle cues that tell how people are feeling about what they are saying. A friend who tells her that she has cancer, for example, may not be asking for a discussion of the relative merits of surgery and chemotherapy. The real "content" here may be her fear and loneliness, and making "cancer" the content misses the point terribly. In talking to Tom at the beginning of this chapter, for example, Libby does not respond to his apparent upset. She stays on task.

This preference for content over context, incidentally, explains why Libby prefers to send an e-mail message to the person in the next office, rather than stand up and walk ten feet. E-mail is a medium that favors content and reduces context to a minimum. Face-to-face interaction is rich in context, and sometimes, Libby feels, the content gets diluted and ignored. When she steps next door to say something, talk becomes chat, and chat seems pointless, a waste of time. Chat is not always pointless, of course. It builds a sense of connection and loyalty, for example, and there are patterns that use chatting as the core of their work. Chatting will never be the core of Libby's work, but she does need to see that chatting, politics, and personal issues serve important functions, setting the context in which they must work. TDF managers have difficulties understanding that tasks have a human context and that the people need as much attention as the task. Cultivating, motivating, recognizing, reassuring, and supporting the people around them seems foreign and suspect. None of this feels like "real work." Libby has become a successful manager because she constantly reminds herself of this vulnerability and works to compensate for it, but no one is ever going to call her a great people manager.

Libby knows this and accepts this. She knows that she is uncomfortable when her people bring personal problems to her at work. "I'm not their mother," she'll say to her friends. She is comfortable when she can focus on a task and when she can help her people perform. Happily, she has found a place where she can use her strengths. She knows that she is uncomfortable in situations requiring unplanned responses and improvisation, so she has found a job that rewards her planning and preparing. Analysis, planning, and control are her pleasures. She values, enjoys, and loves acting skillfully. This is her center. Spontaneity, silliness, and just hanging out have places in her life as well, but much smaller places. Everything, after all, has its time, and everything has its place. The center of Libby's world is her craft. For Libby, success means that she acts skillfully in her work and in her play, with her friends and with her family. This is who she is.

7

The TFD Pattern

TFDs see a world of objective processes and systems without pressing options or priorities. They see a world of subtle, complex, detailed problems. TFDs are observers, clarifiers, and puzzle solvers.

Ted is a TFD who is a lawyer for a large, regional insurance company. His usual responsibilities are to see that the company complies with the complex and conflicting insurance regulations of the fifteen states in which they operate, but now he is on a special assignment. His company is negotiating to buy a smaller competitor, and Ted is on the due diligence team that is evaluating the other company. They've set up shop in a hotel down the road from the other company's headquarters, and Ted is spending his days meeting with his counterparts and his nights reading files and manuals. He's enjoying the change of responsibilities and scenery, but he's also ready to go home. His head is swimming. Right now, he's talking to his friend Sam, the member of the team from underwriting. Ted says, "I don't see how we can possibly report in ten days. Perhaps we should ask for another two weeks. I would never have believed how much information has to be sorted through here. We need two more weeks for that and then ten days to write the report."

Sam shakes his head while he yawns and stretches. "No. That's not going to happen. Better be grateful for the ten days.

Rumors are already affecting both stocks. Nobody expects you to cover everything. We'll do that later. Just find the land mines. Are their people being helpful?"

"Sure," Ted replies. "Their attorneys want this sale to go through. There's just too much to learn so fast. There are so many places to hide your land mines. There are dozens of pending suits that could blow up, there's legislation in Missouri that I don't like, there are problems in their claims procedures, and I don't like their refusals. And that's just scratching the surface. The more we dig, the more we'll find."

"That would be true anywhere, Ted," Sam says. "Come on. I want to go home Friday night. Next week, we'll pull it together. You can only do what you can do."

"I don't like it," Ted says slowly. "If we're going to do this, we should do it right. We need to know what we're getting into here, and I don't think we know. This is a big deal. I spend more time than this buying a new car."

* * * * *

TFD is an observant and thoughtful pattern, describing people like Ted who act quietly, carefully, and patiently, who probe thoughtfully into each task to grasp its complexities and subtleties and to sense the impact of different courses of action. Ted sees a world that is complex and difficult, and he handles this complexity and difficulty with skill and with grace. He observes and clarifies the complexity of the world. We've described TFDs earlier as reflective, reserved, precise, cautious, complex, and patient, but to understand Ted you must move past what you can see and understand his world, a world in which his quiet and thoughtful actions are both sensible and effective.

Ted sees the world as a set of objective processes and systems that create complex and detailed experiences. Imagine that you are watching the workings of an old-fashioned clock, with an elaborate mesh of interlocking gears translating the tension of the tightly wound spring into the precisely timed movement of the clock's hands. Or imagine that you are looking inside your computer or inside your car's engine, tracing the actions of these machines. This gives a sense of the TFD world: intricate, detailed, and interlocking. To understand this world, you have to study the complexity and the details. To understand the results, you have to unravel the processes that created them. At first glance, experience is confusing and chaotic, but order will slowly emerge. Slowly, the process becomes clear. Facts must be put together, given context and connection, to make sense.

This world is a puzzle. If you are patient, observant, and thoughtful, you will see how the facts fit together and know how it works. Understanding – solving the puzzles – engages Ted. He knows that there is order beneath the chaos. You can put together the puzzle, you can see past the chaos to the true order, and you can see how the pieces fit together, if you are patient and persistent.

Ted worries when people move too quickly. The world is complex and the answers are not obvious. Acting as if things are simple is both laughable and dangerous, because impulsive and rash actions destroy. You don't solve puzzles with bulldozers or dynamite, and you don't fix clocks or computer chips with sledgehammers. Responsible action must be cautious and thoughtful. You succeed when you accept the complexity and wait until you understand, because understanding helps you sail down the river rather than batter yourself against the rocks.

Ted's strengths are his patience, his thoughtfulness, and his acceptance. Processes only reveal themselves over time. What you see before you now is only part of the puzzle, but if you wait, more pieces will be revealed. Answers and solutions are rarely obvious, so thought is required. Events, problems, and people cannot be bullied into simplicity. Ted sees a world that is complex and perplexing, but you can't change this by rash action. You must accept the world on its own perplexing terms. Taking a hammer to a clock doesn't simply damage the pieces; it damages the underlying order of the clockworks. Thoughtless action causes irreparable damage, because it creates chaos and disorder. The cost of mistakes is real.

When Ted buys a car, he knows that he is making a major investment that will have daily impact on his life for several years. A mistake in this purchase will have significant consequences, so Ted will not rush this decision. He won't buy impulsively. Ted will try to find out as much as he can about the available choices; he'll think hard about his options; he'll worry about the costs and consequences of various features and add-ons. Only then will he buy. There are endless possibilities, but most of the possibilities would be bad choices. This is a world where you need to walk carefully, so that you don't get lost.

Ted likes to know what he is doing. He has found he succeeds by observing carefully, clarifying the underlying process, and preparing and practicing his own actions. Preparation and practice are key TFD action skills. We mentioned in an earlier chapter that we've found that many firefighters are like Ted. They spend enormous time preparing and practicing, so that when they arrive at a fire, they will know what they are doing. When Ted has a chance to prepare and practice, he acts with confidence and speed. He acts slowly only when he is uncertain. Ted hates to act from confusion and uncertainty, so he invests in preparing. Before he starts his rental car when he is traveling, he checks the map to be sure he knows the route, he checks the controls to see that he understands them, and he looks around to see where the exit is. Only then does he start the car.

Ted plays in a recreational basketball league, and he loves to practice. He loves to get to the gym early and practice his shots. He loves shoot-arounds before the game. He plays a good game. He has a wonderful 18-foot jump shot, and he sets a terrific pick, but he doesn't enjoy the banging under the basket very much. He loves to play with precision, and there's not much precision in a bunch of hacking fouls. Ted has played a lot of basketball, and he knows what he's doing. He knows the game, and he knows his skills. He certainly plays to win, but the real point is performing well. Ted believes the old line about "it's how you play the game that counts." Some of his teammates tell him that he's not aggressive enough on the court, but he believes that you win by playing well, not by slamming bodies.

Ted has become confident and assured as he has come to understand the value of his approach. When he was younger, he worried that he worried too much, that he spent too much time reflecting, and that he should be more spontaneous and looser. We live in a world that values speed, slogans, and snappy retorts more than thought, observation, and preparation, and Ted has never been good with either slogans or snappy retorts. He's more relaxed now. He just got tired of being told to be more aggressive by people he was outscoring. He likes his thoughtfulness, reflection, and care. He's also realized that others value his approach, as well, that people look to him for his reflections and that people listen to his observations. Bold rhetoric doesn't move Ted. "Damn the torpedoes and full speed ahead" are not the words of a TFD. Ted wants to know where the torpedoes are, and he's decided that his results can speak for themselves. Steady, consistent performance can win the race.

Wanting to practice and prepare seems an obvious choice to Ted, but not everyone shares his preference. Some people see Ted as preferring routine and habit to innovation and improvisation, but Ted sees himself as preferring competency. Ted values expertise. Experts know what they are doing, because they have made the investment in preparation and practice. No one becomes an expert overnight. Ted sees that stability and consistency are required for expertise. When things move too quickly, you can't prepare and you can't know what you're doing. Ted has turned down several job opportunities because they would take him outside his scope. He has worked hard to become an expert in compliance. He enjoys being the one people call. His work on the due diligence team is a nice change of pace, but he's happiest when he is an expert. Ted dislikes abrupt change, because he has invested so much in mastering the old ways. Given a little time, he accommodates changes well, but novelty for the sake of novelty simply appalls him. He wants to understand why the changes are worth his efforts.

Ted distrusts impulse. Impulsive behavior is risky, and he sees risk-taking as foolish and immature. This is not a matter of courage. We've mentioned firefighters, for example, who are certainly brave, but who pride themselves on preparing, rehearsing, and reducing the risks of their dangerous job. Risk taking, to Ted, comes from not knowing what you are doing. Acting on the fly is dangerous, because you can't anticipate all the possible results of your unprepared acts. Ted feels sharply the complexities and potential disappointments of action, the many ways you can go wrong, and this can freeze him. Sometimes he simply sighs and lets life make his choices for him. Sometimes the best choices and the right paths are just not clear enough.

Ted has trouble when the pace becomes too quick, when the ground becomes unsure. Uncertainty confuses and slows him. When others are leaping forward, Ted steps back to get a better look. As he looks at the world, the options and choices don't see clear or sharp to him. There are many options and choices, and this wealth of possibilities can overwhelm him. His patience can slide into passivity and his acceptance of complexity and intricacy can become resignation, a sense of the futility of choosing and acting. When things are happening quickly, he feels that he's just not ready yet. He needs more time; he needs more information; he needs more preparation. Time pressures disrupt Ted. He dislikes deadlines, because he needs time and calm to produce and refine his work. External distractions, pressures, or deadlines upset his careful, detailed work. He works best with stability and consistency, but that's not always possible. Learning to live in a world where certainty is often unattainable is Ted's burden.

Learning to act before he is certain, acting when the results are unsure, is Ted's lifelong challenge.

Ted's hesitation when he is uncertain shouldn't obscure his strengths. One of the extraordinary strengths Ted brings to any task is his concern for the details. Ted cares about the details, because if the details aren't right, nothing works. Think about our clockwork example. If you move a gear a fraction of an inch, or if the gear has one tooth more or one tooth less, the entire clock is worthless. Ted is not obsessive, nor is he immune from boredom, but he respects details, and he is irritated that so many people do not. It does no good to fully comply with Illinois regulations for a policy issued in Wisconsin. When Ted is involved, pieces don't get lost and details don't get neglected.

Ted sees perfection as a standard. This is not "perfectionism" in the neurotic, disabling sense. He just wants to act as precisely as he can see, and this can be a very high standard. In practice, Ted translates this standard, this demand for quality, into an effort to avoid mistakes. Ted see his own mistakes as unacceptable, as failures, so he acts slowly and carefully to minimize errors by planning, rehearsing, testing, and revising, over and over, before acting. He reworks, rethinks, and redrafts. He fine-tunes his actions, projects, and responsibilities right through to completion. Even when he is finished, he often replays and refines his acts in his mind. While Ted's thoroughness and quality impress others, he often disappoints himself. He has trouble being satisfied and content with any act, because he sees how it could have been better.

To others, Ted seems easygoing, pleasant, deliberate, and tolerant. His appreciation of life's complexity makes him sympathetic and broad-minded, good help for people wrestling with problems, but it also makes him hesitate to leap in. He hesitates to advise. He hesitates to tell others what to do, think, or feel. He is an observer, slow to participate and slow to become involved, so he can also seem uninvolved and distant. His friends enjoy his humor and his warmth, but only those who know him well see this side of him. Ted focuses more on understanding than on creating a powerful impression or image. His friends value that: Ted isn't putting on a show. As people come to know him, they strongly sense that Ted has real substance.

Ted commits slowly to actions, causes, goals, or relationships, but once committed, he is articulate and dedicated. He can persuade thoughtfully and act persistently, but he resists imposing his views or desires. He tries to bring others along by taking them through all the steps that he himself took on the path to conviction. Understanding and choices cannot be imposed, he feels; they can only be achieved step by step. Because Ted accepts that there are many paths to understanding and choice, he hesitates to enforce his own paths.

Ted sometimes confuses persuading with explaining. When he's trying to sell a product or a process or an idea, he explains at length. He educates. Ted focuses more on understanding than on results, more on the journey than on the destination. He assumes that when people understand, they will be persuaded and they will buy. People do want to understand, but they want to understand what this has to do with them. They want a personal understanding as well as the impersonal and objective understanding Ted offers. While Ted needs to see that there is more to persuading and selling than impersonal explanations, his explanations are the heart of his credibility and the platform on which his persuasions must rest. Ted evokes trust. People simply believe him.

Ted has a genuine talent for diplomacy. This talent surprised him, but he's come to enjoy using these skills. He has never enjoyed courtroom dramatics, but he's found that he enjoys mediating conflicts. He is patient, he doesn't push, and he accepts that people often move slowly. He is good at getting people to focus on the details, where they can often agree, rather than the points on which they disagree. By winning agreement on the details, he builds a sense of agreement and a sense of momentum toward more agreement. He avoids dramatics, he avoids lines in the sand, he avoids slogans, he avoids personal and emotional language, and he avoids simplifying and caricaturing people's positions. People like to feel understood and respected, and this is the heart of his diplomacy.

Ted is articulate, fluent, deliberate, and measured in his speech. Because his messages are complex, he relies on complex words and elaborate verbal constructions. He isn't trying to be impressive or intellectual; he's trying to be accurate and sensitive. Ted sees a rich, elaborate, and complex world, and he wants to speak of this world in equally rich ways. He uses qualifiers, adjectives, and adverbs to capture the precision of his world. He speaks in paragraphs, not in sound bites. Just as he needs time to absorb what he sees, so he needs time to explain it. Words, ideas, and concepts are important to Ted, because only complex ideas can capture the complexity of his reality, but his language can become so complex that he fails to communicate. "Ted," his friends will say, "you're talking like a lawyer again." Then Ted laughs and tries to speak English. Experts sometimes try to say too much. They try to say everything. Ted was horrified when he first took a class in presentation skills, because he thought they wanted glitz without content. He's slowly learning, however, that simplifying helps him communicate. One danger of expertise is trying to explain everything, like the instructions on an IRS form. Details can obscure the point.

TFDs may be the best traditional students. Ted is comfortable in classrooms and lectures, absorbing information, occasionally discussing or debating, and moving step by step through a defined area of study. He enjoyed law school. He liked studying the cases and trying to make sense of their legal process and structure. He liked the precision of the vocabulary. He liked learning to observe through this discipline. His first years practicing law were much more difficult because learning while doing, learning on the fly, is difficult for him. Learning by doing involves making mistakes and feeling inept. Ted wants to know before he acts. He dislikes discussion and interaction as learning tools. Whenever he attends a corporate training session, Ted hopes that he'll see a good, competent expert who will give a good, competent lecture. He doesn't need to hear a bunch of people who don't know anything discuss their ignorance. He doesn't want to be pressured to discuss topics he doesn't fully grasp. He learns by absorbing, not by acting or interacting. Ted mixes these periods of observing and absorbing information with periods of reflection, thought, daydreams, and fantasy in which he works on the information in his head. These imaginary actions, dialogues, and monologues are great assets. At his best, these fantasies are rehearsals, although at other times these fantasies substitute for reality and action. Ted's internal life is remarkably rich. Much of his life is inside his head.

Ted is often described as a loner. He even thinks of himself this way, but this is wrong. He needs time alone, but he also needs people. Ted needs human contact. He sometimes fools himself into believing that he is a loner who doesn't need others, but when he's isolated and forced to work, act, or live alone, Ted does poorly. One reason for this, beyond the real pleasures of companionship, is that Ted uses others to bring him out of his interior life into the world. Balancing his interior and exterior life is crucial to Ted's effectiveness. Too much interior life leads him to rely on fantasy for satisfaction, while too much exterior life leaves him feeling overwhelmed and unsure of himself. He needs both time alone to absorb and time with others to participate.

While Ted enjoys people, he does best where he can feel prepared, where he knows what to expect. He prefers structured, predictable situations built around common interests. He feels clumsy when he must respond quickly to new situations, when he must improvise or make quick judgments. Ted prefers situations where he feels prepared, where he has rehearsed. These are skills that are indispensable in the complex TFD world. Becoming a skilled TFD always means practicing and extending practice and rehearsal to new areas of action. There was a time when this approach was more valued. Social skills used to be carefully taught and rehearsed. One took lessons in dining, dancing, and conversing with strangers. Changing fashions have put Ted at a disadvantage in a social world that values spontaneity and impulse more than propriety and preparation. Ted's best choice, he has found, is to ignore this change in fashions and to prepare and rehearse his social life just as he does his work, so Ted spends time rehearsing interactions in his mind and replaying them until he gets them right.

Most of Ted's friendships are built around shared interests and activities, which give a comfortable structure to his interactions. As you might expect, Ted moves toward intimacy slowly and only after giving himself a chance to observe and get to know the other person in a variety of settings. Ted does not take great social risks, any more than he takes other risks. He also values stability and consistency in his relationships. He doesn't want surprises and excitement, at least as a primary theme. Ted sometimes wishes that he was more outgoing, more spontaneous, but in truth, he prefers his own way. Spontaneity looks rather shallow.

Ted's careful and quiet listening is one of his great strengths, a social skill of the first order, but even skills can be misunderstood. Sometimes people read Ted's quiet listening as lack of interest. Ted doesn't want to respond before he understands, but people see this lack of response as a lack of interest. People have told Ted that he's difficult to read, that it's hard to know how he's reacting to things, that he looks disengaged. He's trying to do better. He works at signaling his interest, by nodding, smiling, and paraphrasing, and he tries to encourage the speaker as well as absorb the speaker's words. This hasn't been easy, but he's found that it helps people feel that he is listening.

Ted spends much time in self-examination and reflection. He observes himself as well as the world. Because Ted absorbs before he expresses, he is slow to express his feelings. He's not holding back; he's simply sorting through how he feels. His reactions to events are complex, and he's confused by how others can respond so quickly. It doesn't feel quite real; it seems too easy. Ted is sensitive to his own inner life and to that of others, and he works to disentangle the complexities of human psychology. His sensitivity is a strength, but in the past it has trapped him in self-consciousness and self-analysis. It's hard to act when you're watching yourself. He's become less self-conscious as he's learned to focus outside himself while he's acting, to look more at the audience and less at his notes when he speaks, to focus on the basket and not his shooting mechanics when he shoots a jump shot.

Still, Ted often feels clumsy and has trouble seeing how positively others view them. People see him as accepting, understanding, tolerant, companionable, and a good listener, as a team player and a good colleague. Ted inspires trust. When he speaks, people believe him. Thought and care are important social strengths. We live in a strange and distorted world when we don't recognize these strengths. Somehow, thoughtfulness becomes a social liability in a world that only sees being gregarious and outgoing as social skills.

Ted prefers groups that focus on tasks rather than talk. In work groups, Ted is seen as a terrific colleague, both helpful and reliable. He's a great team player. Unless the group is focused on a specific content or topic that he knows well, Ted finds himself being silent and simply observing. People regard Ted as quiet because he speaks deliberately and precisely, not spontaneously and enthusiastically. Ted is quiet because he listens before he speaks. He rarely breaks in before others are finished, rarely interrupts, or prompts, or distracts. Quick, back-and-forth exchanges are difficult for him. As we've said, he needs time both to listen and to speak. He often finds himself preparing to say something, but by the time he is ready to speak, the discussion has moved on. In a few groups, people have learned to recognize the look of "getting ready to speak" on Ted's face, and then someone will ask whether he has something to add. Ted finds this helpful. Most often, however, he's content to simply try to track the discussion and absorb what others are saying.

We've already mentioned that Ted was great diplomatic abilities. He's very useful in dealing with conflicts. He establishes clear ground rules and boundaries to minimize and contain conflicts. He's uncomfortable when conflicts become personal or emotional, and he's found that ground rules help prevent that. He prefers building agreement to slugging it out and this is a great gift he brings to his groups. Ted values stability and consistency in his social life, just as he does across the rest of his life.

We're seeing a consistent set of themes. We've stressed the complexity of Ted's world, but Ted has learned a straightforward set of approaches to this complexity – preparation, practice, and rehearsal. These skills apply, he has learned, to all of his actions, his learning, and his social life. He performs best in settings that let him act from these strengths: settings that give him the time to observe and prepare; settings that allow him to develop his skills and expertise; settings that provide some stability and consistency. Ted enjoys challenges and changes best when he has time to prepare for them.

Ted loves specific, structured tasks with clear boundaries, because these are the tasks that allow understanding, the tasks that can be solved. A task that is too large, unbounded, or vague can be overwhelming and unsatisfying. While Ted will mull over the meaning of life, he is happier with better-defined puzzles, puzzles with answers and solutions. Within these boundaries, the more intricate the task, the more intrigued Ted will be. Ted has been fortunate to find settings that value his thoughtfulness and his attention. This is not always easy in a world that values speed and constant motion. Ted has had to struggle to establish, even in his own mind, that these are not the only values that matter, but this struggle has been well worth winning.

8

The FTD Pattern

FTDs see a world of unity and harmony without sharp contrasts or pressing choices. They see a world that demands nurture, attention, and care. They are facilitators and developers.

Anna is an FTD and the head of corporate communications for a major computer hardware company. As she leaves a meeting, Sean catches up with her. Sean runs the product design teams for the company. "You were quiet in there, Anna," he laughed.

"Well, there was a lot to hear and think about," Anna replied, "and it wouldn't have done much good to try to say anything, because no one was listening."

"You're right there," Sean laughed, "it got pretty raucous. But what do you think? Moving manufacture offshore would certainly create a PR nightmare for you to manage."

"If it's the right thing to do, we'll manage the PR," said Anna, "but is it the right thing?" Sean rattled on as they walked back across the campus to their offices, while Anna listened and nodded. As they parted, Anna said, "You know Sean, you should really talk to Tony Marshall. I think you and he could be helpful to each other on this one."

Anna returned to her office and looked over her meeting notes, thought a moment, and then made several phone calls to people who had been at the meeting, just to check in. She sat quietly for a few minutes, thinking about the calls, and then she began her tour of her department. She carried her cup of coffee as she moved from desk to desk, chatting with each person, checking on his or her families and on their projects. This was the most important part of her day, she thought. This was where she could get a sense of how things were moving, who needed help, and what kind of help they needed. Sandy, for example, was sounding bored with her work, so perhaps it was time to juggle assignments to get her interested again. Ken and Martin were complaining about each other, so she'd have to do something about that. And Tina could probably help with the problems Andrea was having.

* * * * *

As an FTD, Anna sees a world of unity, a world of relationships. In this world, nothing happens in isolation. If you touch one strand of the web, every strand quivers. Anna sees her world as if it were a forest or a garden that will thrive and flourish with careful balance and thoughtful harmony. Biological imagery seems inescapable with FTDs. Anna experiences the world as a living, evolving, and growing place, as an ecology where the parts fit together and support and nourish one another. If you prefer, think of Anna as an old-fashioned family doctor, sensing the interplay of environment, stresses, diet, exercise, genetics, family relationships, health practices, and much more in shaping the health of every patient. Every piece tells a story, and every story brings together many pieces. Understanding and helping her patients means seeing how these pieces connect and how these connections shape the patient sitting before her.

Anna is puzzled when people talk about simple choices or black and white distinctions or a narrow focus on the bottom line. Anna's world is more complex, like an old-fashioned dance where the partners and the patterns are constantly moving and weaving. If you focus too closely, you can't see the pattern. Every piece is important. "For want of a nail, the shoe was lost; for want of a shoe, the horse was lost; for want of a horse, the message was lost; for want of the message, the battle was lost; and for want of the battle, the kingdom was lost." All great successes bring together many small pieces. The bringing together is the success. You cannot simply seize one piece and proclaim "This is the key." Every piece might be a key, because every piece is connected to every other piece.

How should you act in this contextual, relational, interdependent world? How should you act in a world in which every piece has connections and the connections have consequences? We've said in earlier chapters that FTDs are warm, gentle, and sympathetic. We've described their work style as team-oriented, cooperative, and harmonizing and their communication as receptive, sensitive, and inclusive. We must, however, move deeper to understand Anna's world, a world in which warmth, cooperation, and sensitivity are powerful and effective ways to act. We like the image of the gardener here. A gardener brings together the elements that will become the garden – the seeds, the soil, the water, and the sun – and then waits, watches, and tends. When potentially disruptive forces emerge, such as weeds, bugs, or diseases, she acts to correct the balance. A garden calls for constant attention and constant tending. Acting in this world requires *care*, because balances and harmonies are easily disrupted, and consequences take time to develop. This world rewards patience and care.

Anna acts carefully and patiently. She values attending and tending to her world, and she distrusts both the thoughtless and the impatient. She values careful attention, because the relationships between events reveal themselves only subtly and slowly, in hints, intimations, and whispers. In her world, nudges are more effective than shoves and walking will carry you further and let you see more than sprinting. She pays attention to connections and she nurtures connections. She connects people who can help each other, and she separates people who hurt each other. She coordinates actions so they support each other and don't interfere with each other. She fits ideas or images or concepts to events to help people understand better. When she speaks with you, she is not informing you, she is connecting to you. She creates environments. She helps bring things together.

Anna has become strong and assured as she has found how effective she can be. She chooses to work in the background, behind the scenes, outside the spotlight, because this indirect style works better in her world than pushing or demanding or taking center stage. She is not quiet because she is shy or frightened. She is quiet because it allows her to see and hear better. When she compares herself to more flamboyant or more aggressive people, she sometimes wonders why she can't be the star. But in the end, flamboyance and aggression seem pointless and even destructive. Subtle and quiet acts are more powerful, she believes. She doesn't stir the waters, but she guides the stream.

Sometimes Anna seems to take care of others more than of herself. Sometimes this is true, but Anna believes that what helps others will also help her, so she does not see herself as sacrificing her own interests. She doesn't see herself as noble. Asking Anna to practice "healthy selfishness" or "look out for number one" is pointless. A mature FTD like Anna has learned to care for herself by first caring for the entire system.

Anna acts carefully, even tentatively, because she knows that results are difficult to foresee. Every action creates ripples that can reach far away, and abrupt or thoughtless action is more likely to destroy than to build. The phrase "first do no harm," from the physician's Hippocratic Oath, reflects a deep FTD conviction. It's better to do nothing than to do harm. Sometimes, however, this conviction leads to inaction and passivity where simple, bold action might serve better. A growth point for Anna has been learning that pruning and surgery are sometimes necessary. Punishing and disciplining, asserting, imposing, and pushing, for example, are difficult for Anna. She has trouble pushing her people when deadlines are pressing. She has trouble reprimanding an employee who is repeatedly late. She even has trouble giving an employee a poor evaluation. She knows that these are skills she needs, at least in emergencies. She also has the nagging sense, however, that these are her failures. If she had managed better the deadline wouldn't press so hard, if she had helped the late employee see the reasons for punctuality then the problem would have dissolved, and if she had coached better, the poor employee would have performed better. Anna, as you can see, is hard on herself. Her first impulse is generally to blame herself for any failings in her world.

These difficulties, however, should not obscure Anna's powerful strengths. People respond to Anna's engagement, care, and acceptance, feeling the warmth and concern in her attention and her interest. Anna always has time to listen, to talk, and to interact. She remembers birthdays and special occasions and loves to celebrate them. She brings thoughtful gifts for no special reason. She drops a note if she hasn't heard from someone for a time. She remembers people's children and families, their joys and their sorrows. People seek Anna when they are troubled and simply want to talk, without advice, judgment, or opinions, or when they want to celebrate, without jealousy, second-guessing, or one-upping. People trust Anna to care.

This style is not always valued in the aggressive world of American business. Anna is sometimes ignored and treated as if she were invisible because she acts unobtrusively and carefully, but her presence has impact. While excitement seekers and adventurers may see her as too cautious, and the number crunchers and data analysts may mock her as too soft, Anna patches the damage her critics inflict. In the hurly-burly of American culture, patience can be confused with passivity. Anna is not passive. She heals, soothes, and restores people's spirits and worlds. She builds for the long run.

Her sense of building for the long run is the wellspring of her patience. She knows that the future grows from the soil of the present and that you cannot leap from planting the seed to picking the fruit. Solid results require solid foundations. Anna knows that change is part of life, but she distrusts dramatic change, change that is not well rooted and well supported. Change cannot be arbitrary and capricious if it is to take root in the ground that has already been prepared. Anna's distrust of dramatic change becomes her contribution to her organization, paradoxically, when dramatic change is underway. Anna is not swept up in the drama and insists on clear communication, attention to detail, and broad participation to stabilize the organization. Anna's concerns and skills are invaluable in giving the changes permanency and restoring stability, coherence, and identity to the changing system. Many organizational changes fail because they ignore the significance of these contributions.

Anna is often pigeonholed as "good with people" or "people-people," but this oversimplifies her contributions. People will say, "Yes, Anna does a good job; everybody likes her," as if being liked is her primary talent. Anna is not limited to the "people stuff." She works skillfully, and she learns skillfully. She brings the same talent for seeing complexity, relationship, and connections to every area of her life. She brings the same patience, insight, and care to her work that she brings to her relationships with people. Anna coordinates beautifully, for example, fitting pieces together so that complex work gets done smoothly. She has responsibility in her job for PR, employee newsletters, meeting arrangements, multimedia, and a host of other communication vehicles, produced by a host of temperamental specialists, dependent on external vendors, and responsible to a very sensitive executive committee. She makes it all seem effortless.

She senses how people feel about their work, about each other, and about their environments. She has a great sense of customer and how to tailor products to please them. She has a sense of how audiences will respond to messages. She sees how one piece of work can support another or hinder another. She sees how Tony's work on a display for the headquarters' lobby can contribute to Andrea's work on the annual report. She sees how the United Way campaign might balance rumors that an operations center is going to close. She sees how a meeting planned for New York will drain resources from work in California. She designs communication campaigns that persuade, arranges meetings that succeed, and runs a department so that it is both productive and enjoyable. She has a knack for knowing when things don't fit, when a chair or a person is in the wrong place, or when a work process is poorly designed. She feels she has succeeded when everything fits together smoothly, when chaotic or disarrayed work processes or uncertain and erratic relationships have been brought into harmony and balance. Anna is a brilliant matchmaker, fitting people together, fitting jobs together, and fitting jobs to people.

If you were trying to understand Anna's organization, you would certainly want to talk with Anna. The way she understands the world and the way she works have given her a wealth of information. Any anthropologist would love to have her as an informant. She knows the history of the organization, the personal relationships among the participants, and people's hopes and fears. Anna knows everyone and has heard their stories. She knows where the bodies are buried and who owes what to whom. Anna knows the story. This is one of the great advantages of listening.

When you speak with Anna, however, you need to understand that her images and pictures of the organization resemble impressionist paintings more than realist paintings. She sees patterns and connections, not sharp edges or facts. You can hear this in her explanations. When asked a question, she responds with a story. If you ask her how many people work in her department, she will explain her staffing philosophy and how this particular configuration of jobs came into existence. If you ask her to write a report, she will need to know where it is going and who is going to read it and how it is going to be used. She needs to see things in context, and her great informational skill is building this sense of context, of a larger picture that gives sense to the smaller pieces. Facts in isolation feel lifeless to her.

Similarly, she doesn't see choices as sharp and clear. Her world has very few hard edges. When she hears her colleagues talk about X being the only option, she wonders why they are not considering Y, Z, A, B, and C as well. Choices and options are rarely simple and clear, and the best policy is generally to wait and see how events play out. "It's too soon to judge" is one of Anna's pet phrases. Things will become more clear in time. It's best to look at things from a variety of angles and perspectives, because there may be connections that you are not seeing.

Anna learns best in settings that give her opportunities to observe and reflect from many different perspectives. Although she loves to read, Anna learns better from people than from books. People give her different perspectives and show her different ways of connecting to the information. Her best learning is personal and contextual. Anna doesn't learn facts; she learns stories.

Anna uses information to form impressions, to get a sense of the patterns and connections, and then she remembers the impressions, not the facts. Anna absorbs large amounts of information in this process, and she can feel overwhelmed by a sense of overload, of too much. She frequently needs to back away to reflect and just let the information soak in. Anna doesn't catalogue, cross-reference, or index information. She simply soaks it in and lets the meanings slowly emerge. She withdraws to ruminate and think and absorb.

Anna needs to connect new information with what she already knows, so she spends lots of time remembering. The past is always present for Anna, because the present is simply one

moment in the intertwined patterns that make up life. Reminisc-
ing allows her to connect new moments with old moments, to
connect new stories to old stories. Old friends, old places, old
experiences are cherished and kept present. This is again part of
her sense of the long term, of the long run. Novelty has little
appeal for Anna. Stability, constancy, and harmony are much
more appealing to her, and this is central to her learning. She is
seeking consistency and continuity.

Both in her working and in her learning, Anna works best in
groups. She sees groups as opportunities to build mutual support
and reinforcing perspectives. Groups potentially bring together a
much richer sense of connection than any one person could.
Anna values this sense of mutual support in groups, but she is
also sensitive to the risks of conflict and disruption that groups
engender. The FTD talent for groups is based on managing these
risks.

Anna builds cohesion within a group, a sense of connection
and belonging, by forging a group identity, a sense of "who we
are." When making business decisions, for example, Anna's
question is always, "Is this the sort of thing that a company like
us should do? Do these acts fit who we are?" This is a powerful
question that other people neglect to their cost. This sense of
identity drives personal commitments to the group's actions.
Many team-building efforts in corporate America are attempts,
often clumsy, to build this FTD sense of group identity. Anna
doesn't need consultants, facilitators, mugs, sweatshirts, and
posters, however, to build identity. She moves one person, one
relationship, at a time to build common ground and shared pur-
pose. She may not be the most visible member of groups, but no
one is more central.

Groups with Anna as a member work more smoothly and effectively, because she builds harmony, cohesion, and mutual support. Anna reduces tension and conflict by moving people into
awareness of their common ground and shared purposes. "I

know that you two disagree," she will tell a friend, "but don't forget that you two share so much. You are friends. You have history. Let's keep this in perspective." Putting things in perspective, putting things in context, is a great FTD talent.

This is not magic, nor is it necessarily benign and saintly. This is politics, and Anna has a flair for politics. When we think of politics in America, we usually think of politicians giving speeches and seeking election. This is not Anna. The thought of giving speeches appalls her. Anna's politics is more parliamentary. She builds alliances; she promotes participation; she instills commitment. She nudges and she hints, then she gets others to nudge and hint. She maneuvers people so that they don't even know that they've been maneuvered. She will cheerfully surrender credit or ownership of the project, if your sense of credit and ownership works in her favor. Her trick is persisting without pestering and her best tools are alliances, favors, and personal loyalties. We joke with those who underestimate the power of FTDs that you can test this power by trying to fire an FTD subordinate. You will create uproar. People will threaten to quit in protest; your peers will refuse to talk to you; the chairman of the board will be on the phone. Only then will you realize the invisible power of FTD, how she has made herself indispensable and irreplaceable.

Anna influences through intimacy. She builds relationships and uses these relationships to shape events. FTDs influence quietly, slowly, and carefully. Anna doesn't seek intensity, fire, and passion; she seeks depth and permanence. This is true throughout her life, because her life is not divided into compartments. Her life is built on connections. The people she works with are her friends. You notice suddenly one day that you are good friends with an Anna without knowing when or how this happened, although you are happy that it has. Anna builds friendships by thinking of people, reflecting on their needs and desires, making contact, doing favors, and staying in touch. Anna builds relationships to last.

Anna likes to claims that she cannot sell, but she sells brilliantly. She sells by fitting and tailoring the product to the customer. A good image here is retail sales at its best, where the goal is to please the customer so that the customer will return, where the goal is to form a permanent relationship with the customer. Anna would not sell a customer anything that is not right for him, but she may very well know better than the customer what fits him. This type of selling takes time, especially in the beginning. Anna must get to know the customer and the customer's problems, tastes, and resources. There is no good way to script this process or hurry it along. The reward is in repeat business. Customers feel well served and come back. When we complain about customer service in our hurried world, and idealize and romanticize the past, this is the image we are using as our standard.

While Anna values harmony and cooperation, she can be tough and even brutal with those who violate her sense of "how we act and who we are." Remember that this sense is at the core of group identity and commitment for her. These are not light matters, because they hurt the group. Her first step is to express disappointment. The power of her disappointment is real; parents have used this tactic for hundreds of generations to inspire guilt and obedience. If this personal appeal fails, she mobilizes the group against the violator, creating peer pressure to bring the offender back in line. If even this isn't enough, she uses the ultimate FTD punishment, banishing the offender from the group. If you will not be one of us, then you cannot be one of us.

Anna, however, prefers inclusion to exclusion. She values relationships and only relinquishes them with hesitancy and regret. She has trouble letting go of relationships even when those relationships are dying or destructive. She's invested too much time, energy, and care to relinquish her efforts lightly, so she may find herself tolerating relationships in which she is being used, neglected, or even abused, hoping that the relationship will heal if she just hangs in. This is admirable until it becomes stupid, and Anna can have trouble knowing when she's crossed the line from caring into stupidity.

Although Anna has a strong group orientation, she prefers to talk with one person at a time so she can feel a direct connection. Anna is a wonderful listener, but she also loves to talk. She communicates by telling stories, because stories can carry the complexity of what she sees. Stories also build personal connections. "You and I are connected," she is saying, "not only because we work in the same department, but because we both love our children, we both love Paris, we both feel guilty about being so busy, and we both think baseball is boring." These connections are what her stories are about.

Sometimes, however, people have trouble grasping the point of her stories and become impatient and tune her out. And sometimes, to be honest, her stories don't have a point. Often, however, there is a point. Anna may try to tell an employee that he is in trouble by telling a story about a time when she was having difficulties on the job. Not everyone can pick up on these subtle messages. Anna thinks that a good story will convey its own conclusion, its own moral, but sometimes it would help if she would draw the conclusion more bluntly. Similarly, she sometimes listens too patiently, apparently in the belief that if she listens long enough, the other person will eventually say something meaningful. Would that this were true!

Because of her concern for disrupting relationships, Anna acts subtly and values gentleness. She monitors, filters, and censors what she says to cushion and protect the other person. She means this to be thoughtful, but she needs to know that people may experience this as evasive and even dishonest. Anna may use encouraging words and lavish praise for the minor successes of a failing employee when straight talk would be more helpful and truly kinder. One of our favorite FTDs likes to say that you catch more flies with honey than with vinegar, but he is ignoring the many uses of vinegar. Anna believes that her negative feedback can be heard between the lines of her positive words, but not everyone listens so subtly. Anna doesn't always realize that not everyone listens as carefully and thinks so intently as she does.

Sometimes, Anna listens too hard. She replays conversations in her mind and ruminates on them. She worries about what people are "really" saying. She sometimes reads between the lines when there is only blank paper between the lines. She can worry for days about a friend not saying "hello" in passing in the hallway, when that friend may simply have been distracted. She can take things personally that were not meant to be personal. Sometimes, her sensitivity is a mixed blessing.

Out of her concern, Anna is a superb listener, but she also needs time to absorb and digest the message, fit it into context, and form a response that addresses the full richness of the message. She is uncomfortable when pushed to a quick reaction that cannot honor the many layers in what she is hearing. In one-to-one interactions, Anna responds slowly, so when you speak with her, you must give her the moment of silence that she needs to formulate a response. In larger groups, Anna is generally quiet, because trying to understand and address the needs of many people simultaneously is so difficult. She'll wait until later and speak with everyone individually. Anna does not respond quickly, but she responds with care.

We started by describing FTDs as a quiet pattern, and we hope you understand that quietness better now. Anna is quiet precisely because so much is going on. A world as complex and rich as Anna's does not encourage rash words or hasty actions. Anna works best in situations that require team efforts, in which time and production quantity are not major pressures, where opportunities for some artistry, creativity, and group expressiveness are possible, and where a cooperative, congenial pattern of relationships is valued. Sadly, modern business disdains these values, to its cost. Anna has learned to accept the instabilities of modern life, but she has also learned that she needs to build islands of stability and constancy for herself, both inside and outside her work. She has also learned that the connections she builds can outlast jobs and even corporations. She does indeed build for the long run.

9

The FDT Pattern

FDTs see a world of unity, with limited facts, order, or stability. They see a kaleidoscopic world of interactions. FDTs are experiencers and expressers.

Alex is an FDT who works as a regional manager for a national chain of retail stores. Now he's doing the two things he knows best: he's on the road and he's on the phone. He's talking to the manager of the store he'll visit tomorrow while on his way to another meeting. His phone leaves his hands free to drive and to sort through the papers in the open briefcase on the next seat. He's just told the store manager a funny story about his daughter's soccer game last weekend and even while he's still laughing, he says "Look, Frank, you guys are doing great. I love you guys, because you make my job so easy. We both know you've got some issues, but you're still one of my top stores, and I love you. I want you to be my top store, though, and I can't see why you aren't. So I'm going to be all over you about your jewelry department. With your location, you should be doing better there. You've got an opportunity staring your in the face."

He listens for a moment as he pulls his cola from the drink holder and checks the speedometer. Then he says, "Look, let's build my visit around this jewelry thing. I mean, I'll run around the store and say 'hi" to everyone, but let's really focus here. Let's get your jewelry people into your office and let's get them fired up." He rummages in his briefcase, balancing the drink against the steering wheel. "I've got some presentation materials here that show sales at other locations. Let's use these numbers to show these people what they ought to be doing. And I've got a memo here from our jewelry buyer about your ordering patterns. She doesn't like them."

He listens again as he begins watching the signs so he can gauge where he is on the road. "You may be right," he says, "Maybe Libby's not right for this job. Give me some time with her, why don't you?"

He listens again and laughs, "Yes, yes, and yes. Hey look, I'm about ten minutes away for Cynthia's store. You think I'm tough on you. You really wouldn't want to be her today. Let me change ground real quick. Have you got this award dinner stuff lined up for tomorrow night?"

* * * * *

As an FDT, Alex sees a world that is fluid, colorful, dramatic, and exciting, a world of swirling patterns and unities. He sees a world of connections and relationships in constant motion, like the colored pieces of glass in a kaleidoscope, tumbling into new unities with each twist of the tube. People, objects, tasks, and ideas all enter this swirling mix, as one unity tumbles and dissolves into another unity. Alex is fascinated and absorbed by this world. The richness of this world can be grasped only by engaging and participating, not by observing or analyzing. The world is not something that is happening "out there." You are part of it; you are connected to it; you touch events and events touch you. As soon as you try to disentangle these patterns, break them into their components, you lose their reality. Engagement and involvement comes first. Life is a participation sport, not a spectator sport.

Alex has trouble understanding people who stand back and observe, people who seem detached and uninvolved. Several of the other regional managers in his company like to stay in their offices and work from reports and numbers, but Alex doesn't see how they can work that way. He has to be out there, talking to employees and customers, seeing the advertising and displays, listening to people's stories. Numbers and reports are useful, but only if he can fit them into a richer context, a richer picture. There is so much going on that he has to see it and touch it or it just feels like chaos. Only when he makes himself part of the picture does it make sense to him. When he tries to stand back and observe, all he sees is confusion.

How should you act in this world of constantly shifting unities and deeply personal patterns? People describe Alex as energetic, outgoing, and spontaneous, and this style fits his world. You must engage this world to make sense of it. In an earlier chapter, we described FDTs as engaged, fun-loving, personal, spontaneous, responsive, participative, facilitative, expressive, dramatic, and involving, but understanding Alex means understanding the world that makes these actions powerful and effective. Alex sees a world in constant motion, a world of shifting patterns. There is little that is objective, enduring, impersonal, or external in his world. Reality is in the moment, in the immediate patterns around him. Reality is personal and immediate; it is right here and it is us. You can't deal with this world by standing back and observing, so Alex plunges in.

Alex lives in these personal moments, in the immediate patterns around him, and his great gift is engaging and responding quickly and suitably to the moment. When he is making a presentation at a regional managers' meeting, for example, Alex has a strong sense of "how it's going," and he adjusts and shifts his presentation based on this sense. When he reads a financial report, he jumps around until he finds the numbers that suddenly help him see an issue more clearly. He never knows what those numbers will be or where they will be, but he knows that, with luck, something will click and a new pattern will jump out and make sense. Alex responds to what emerges and takes shape in front of him. He doesn't worry about detailed preparation and planning, because the patterns and shapes are unpredictable. Certainly some planning and preparing is useful, but in the end you react to what you see. He is brilliantly ad hoc.

Alex connects quickly with people, forming quick friendships and relationships. He senses how to connect, how to move past the routine interaction and transform impersonal contact into personal connection. The other person is never just a sales clerk or a friend of a friend or a work associate. All Alex's connections are personal and this openness and interest feels warm and personal, an appealing combination. Connecting is so natural for Alex that talk about "building" relationships sounds a bit strange to him. Relationships happen, and they happen all the time. He finds himself in many important relationships to which he gives time, energy, and loyalty, but this is neither planned nor an effort. Alex loves to walk the halls when he's at corporate headquarters, just to see who's there. He loves to pick up the phone and reconnect with old acquaintances. He's puzzled when others pull back, seeking distance and fixed roles. Distance troubles him; he feels unconnected and unvalued. Connecting is his gift.

Alex seems to live in an endless swirl of people, at the center of a continual carousel of formal and informal groups. From the chaos of getting his family in motion in the morning to the parade of small and large meetings in his office and on the road to the evenings of community activities and phone time with friends, Alex feels he is surrounded. And he loves it. Although he needs time alone, time offstage, time to refocus, Alex draws energy from being with people. He builds time alone into his day to catch up on his paperwork, to read and to reflect, and he values this time, but he never needs to stay alone long. Connecting and being part of people's lives is the core of Alex's life.

His immersion in the moment is Alex's great strength and great weakness. The people he works with call him "dynamic," but he can also seem inconsistent, erratic, and overwhelming. As he shifts from moment to moment, Alex's responsiveness and spontaneity can look and feel inconsistent, unanchored, and flighty. His friends complain that watching Alex is like watching a pinball machine as he bounces from topic to topic and from person to person. He's always in motion. You don't know how long he'll stay or where he'll go next.

The grace and facility with which Alex moves through the world misleads some people into believing that life is just a party for Alex. They don't see his worrying, brooding, and fretting. Where others see grace and facility, Alex may feel overwhelmed and inept. He worries that he is missing the point. Sometimes he is so involved, so close up, that he loses his perspective. He worries about the subtle, the remote, and the unlikely as much as the obvious, the immediate, and the probable. He will worry for hours about a tone of voice, or he will be upset that a waiter didn't respond to his friendliness. He seeks perspective from others by checking that they see things as he has and that his actions seem right. As he has grown, his need for this reassurance has diminished, but he still feels it. The absence of simple, unchanging anchors in his world can leave him feeling out of control and buffeted by every wind.

Alex has learned to step back to take a longer view, applying his keen sense of unity to develop a more stable sense of his actions and his possibilities. Alex has achieved more perspective and stability by anchoring himself in some simple, central values that give his life shape and coherence. He has spent a lot of time thinking about his values, about what is important. In his work in the retail industry, for example, he sees intense customer focus as the key to success and he preaches this gospel at every opportunity. He repeats the phrase "Delight the customer" so often that people laugh when he says it or recite it along with him. Alex laughs as well, but he is absolutely serious. It sounds like a slogan, but it is a way of keeping focus, consistency, and perspective. In his complex world, simply articulating his core values has an almost magical property. He comes back again and again to these expressions of his values and reminds himself of them frequently. His travel mug says "Delight the customer," as does the poster on his office door.

The people around him are keenly aware of Alex's social skills and presence, but they often underestimate his other talents. Alex, however, has wonderful technical skills and expertise. He shows the same gifts for sensing patterns, relationships, and unity in the world of events, machinery, work designs, and the worlds of ideas or art. In his organization, for example, people admire Alex for his "intuitive" grasp of the business. Alex senses quickly when problems are developing that no one else has suspected. Where others see just another fluctuation in sales in a department, Alex sees an opportunity. Alex may notice a group of kids wearing strange clothes and push his clothing buyer toward that fashion. When asked how he knows that there is an opportunity or a new trend, he stumbles a bit and says, "Well, it seemed pretty obvious; anybody could have seen it." But he is the one who saw it. With effort, he could doubtless construct a logical sequence of connections, but that's after the fact and doesn't reflect how he truly knew. The word "intuitive" is unfair because it suggests that this result is somehow effortless and easy, but Alex had to work hard for a long time to know the retail business this well. His effort, however, is not what shows. Alex has to live with this burden. Some people don't take Alex seriously because it just looks too easy.

This is an interesting paradox for Alex. He is a gifted storyteller, but he struggles to articulate his thoughts. He struggles to put into words what he can picture so clearly. Sometimes he feels that he is trying to say everything at once and that it all comes out in a jumble. Alex hates this struggle, because it makes him feel stupid or flighty. He knows that he avoids arguing with people at work who understand the business much less well than he does, because he feels so clumsy in trying to put his understanding into words. He'll joke or tell a story instead. He knows that some of his peers underrate him and think that he's succeeding on style rather than substance. He sees more than he can say.

Alex is more comfortable acting and interacting. Because of his sense of unity and context, of how things fit together, Alex implements brilliantly. He brings plans to life. He has an uncanny sense of how things come together and of the sources of friction and disruption in that process. Chaos and confusion do not intimidate him, and he has the flexibility to juggle tasks, shifting quickly from one to another. He works best when he coordinates, cajoles, harmonizes, and smoothes, and he's brilliant at enlisting and enrolling others as part of this effort. Alex is gifted at drawing people into common efforts, working with people as an artist works with colors. The energy of these interactions charges him. Alex appreciates that what looks simple on the chalkboard is messy and complex in the real world, and he has a talent for bridging this gap. Alex knows how to make changes part of the fabric of life in the organization. He knows that people have to be sold on the changes and given roles in the changes. He knows that plans must be personalized.

On the other hand, Alex has trouble with tasks that feel disconnected, isolated, or out-of-context. If his boss calls and asks for the clerical turnover numbers for one of Alex's stores, Alex's first response is to ask "Why?" He wants to know the context of the request. If asked to look at the numbers for a sales department in a store he doesn't know, he will want to know the manager's history, local demographics, the sales history of the store, and much more. He needs a personal and contextual picture. Performing a task when he doesn't see how that task fits into some larger picture feels arbitrary and pointless to him. He has difficulty tracking disconnected facts or details. Memos, reports, and receipts stay in his in-basket or are lost in a desk drawer if Alex doesn't see how the are connected to him, if he doesn't see the picture they are parts of. Someone who just want an analysis of the numbers may be irritated by his questions, or perhaps even challenged and undermined, but that is not Alex's intention. Acting in a vacuum is very difficult for Alex; his strength, after all, is connections.

Alex also risks over-engaging and over-committing. The risk is that his engagement and action will become disorganization and chaos. Organization and managing detail will never be his strengths. He laughs about how his world is held together by baling wire and duct tape, yet he keeps adding more. He finds himself juggling more and more balls, growing more manic and more frantic as the activity level increases and as the complexity of the tasks grows geometrically. His impulse is to keep moving and to go faster, but the better solution is to disengage, drop some of the balls, step back, look things over, and plan. This can feel impossible to an FDT in action, but Alex has learned to use friends to help him disengage and step back. Learning to delegate has been one of Alex's great triumphs.

The accusation that Alex is all show and no content stings. It has taken Alex many years to realize that he is a smart man. School was a trial for him: they asked him to sit still and be quiet; they made him follow systematic, step-by-step lessons; and they responded to his questions by telling him to wait. The school system seemed committed to making learning as unnatural as possible for Alex. He learns by engaging, by talking, by following his interests and energy where they lead. He learns in groups, not alone. He learns by interacting, not by absorbing and reflecting. Alex knows that he sometimes irritates people in company training programs because he begins asking questions and telling stories as soon as a session begins. He also knows that if he doesn't do this, he'll get nothing from the session. Alex is looking for connections, patterns, and unities when he is learning. He loves to see sudden connections; he loves the "aha" of insight. He loves the moments when he can say, "Yes, yes, yes; now I see it." These moments, however, are elusive and impossible to program. Step-by-step, cumulative learning is the struggle. It just doesn't resonate. When he teaches, Alex tries to deliver the kinds of insights and excitement that he values, though many of his trainees wish he would pay more attention to the basics.

Alex is a storyteller. When asked for an explanation, Alex tells a story. When asking for an explanation, Alex wants a story. Alex could just tell his managers to watch their employee turnover, but he feels he has communicated better if he tells them about how he reduced turnover by 20% in his first store by talking to his people and then changing his scheduling practices. He can read sales figures, but they aren't alive for him until he has heard the salespeople tell their stories. Then the numbers become meaningful. Stories provide the framework that gives facts meaning and depth. "So what's the story?" is how Alex greets a manager coming to him with a problem. "Let me tell you a story" is how he begins his answer. Alex thinks in metaphors and in impressions, not in facts or concepts, and stories carry the kind of information that is most useful for him. Stories also help Alex engage other people and connect with them. Communicating is not simply relaying information; it is building connections. Alex involves people, interests them, makes them feel important and valued, and builds a sense of participating and sharing.

Alex's stories can also confuse and irritate people. Sometimes Alex communicates more than the other person wants, needs, or can assimilate. Not everyone shares Alex's passion for context, and people sometimes hear Alex's stories as pointless chatter and tune him out. They're waiting for the information they value, such as facts, choices, decisions, or procedures. Since he focuses on building connection, he sometimes forgets about relaying simple, impersonal information about the world. Sometimes all that needs to be said is "I'll be there at seven," without a detailed discussion of how he is traveling and with whom he is traveling.

When listening, Alex doesn't focus on the content. He listens for the connections between what is said, how it is said, who is saying it, and the context in which that person is speaking. Even the simplest communication contains all these layers, and a communication that lacks these layers feels empty. It was probably an FDT who first began adding facial expression symbols to e-mail – you know, those things that look like :) :(:/ - because e-mail is impoverished in communicating social context. Alex is not a quiet listener: he engages; he draws out, he encourages; he becomes part of the story. He can have difficulty hearing impersonal messages, and he can be oversensitive to unintended overtones or implications in others' messages. Being handed a copy of the corporate dress code is not always a comment on your personal attire. Alex can read too much into messages; he can be too sensitive.

Alex has learned that he has difficulty focusing on the simple content of what he is hearing because he is attending to so much. He's learned that when he has important decisions to make, he does better if the information is on paper, where he can focus on the content. Alex does well with content, when he can isolate it and focus on it. This has been a very useful lesson.

Groups seem to form spontaneously around Alex. His office and his home are hubs of activity. Alex is on the school board; he's on the coordinating committee for youth soccer in his community, and he's active in several church groups. People sought him for each of these activities, and Alex has trouble saying no. People see Alex as a leader because people are attracted to him and he is widely liked. Alex doesn't see himself as a leader, however; he sees himself as a facilitator, as someone who helps people do what needs to be done. "I'm not a leader," he'll say, "I'm just good at getting other people to do the work."

Alex *is* good at getting other people to do the work. One of his great talents is recruiting, finding people who will do the job and attracting them to their roles within a team. "I don't know anyone who's as good as you with print advertising," he'll say to one of his managers and that manager becomes a print advertising advisor to his other managers. "I bet you would really enjoy helping this committee; they're good people, and they really could use your help," he'll say to a new church member. He sees were people will fit and he brings them onto his team. He recruits and he motivates. He makes jobs seem exciting and important. "Stuffing these envelopes is really going to help our kids by letting folks know what their choices are." He also motivates people by encouraging their sense of friendship and loyalty to him. He excels at asking people to help *him*. And people want to help him. The roles he plays are encourager, recruiter, mediator, and supporter. The group norms he supports are "be a friend," "think of others," and "participate."

Alex wants people to get along, and he wants people to enjoy their interactions with him, and he sees conflict as disrupting these relationships. His task during conflict is rebuilding and reasserting relationships. "I know you and John disagree over this issue, but I need for you and John to work together. I need for us to be a team. Do you think you can put this aside for now and give me a hand?" He stresses loyalties, connections, and alliances. He pushes people to understand one another's viewpoints, to understand. He creates pressure for cooperation. Alex can be direct and confrontational when he sees core values being risked, but his preference is always to build cooperation and agreement.

Alex's skills in recruiting and motivating are important political skills, but people often overestimate Alex's political acumen. On several painful occasions, Alex has been badly hurt in political struggles he didn't even recognize. At a previous job, for example, he got caught in the middle of a power struggle between his boss and his boss's boss because he didn't see that his boss's boss was using him as an information source. Alex can be too trusting. One of his friends later said to him, "You just

couldn't believe that he didn't really want to be your friend."
That's true; Alex assumes people like him and want to do well
by him. In this case, it cost him his job and taught him something about discretion. Alex also has trouble sometimes when he
tries to please different people and ends up being accused of being inconsistent and talking out of both sides of his mouth. This
isn't fair, perhaps, but Alex is slowly learning that he is vulnerable to this perception.

For Alex, experience is personal, interactive, and involving,
and this gives him a great "audience sense," a sensitivity to how
people are reacting and responding. Alex is a performer. He loves
an audience. He thinks carefully about how to dress, about how
to present himself, about the images he is creating. He works to
draw people to him, to engage them, to interest them, and to
involve them. He has a strong sense of how he affects people,
and he will junk a prepared script instantly if it isn't connecting
to the audience. He attends carefully to his impact on people. He
feels their comfort and their discomfort, their approval and their
disapproval, their interest and their lack of interest. This is a
great strength, but sometimes he sacrifices content to please an
audience. Alex knows that his urge to please his audience is both
seductive and risky. He hesitates to upset, and he hesitates to go
further than others are willing to go. When he senses that other
people are uncomfortable, he becomes uncomfortable. He knows
where the line is. He enjoys his audiences too much to risk of-
fending them.

Alex's ability to connect is a powerful source of his influence
with people. He fits the classic image of the salesman, and he
likes to claim that he can sell anything. One of his best friends,
however, once told him, "Alex, you only know how to sell one
thing, and that's Alex." There's some truth here. You buy from
Alex, in part, because you like him. His persuasiveness is personal. This is a great strength in sales and other forms of influence, but there are vulnerabilities here as well. He may spend

more time, for example, building relationships than building a case. While Alex connects quickly, he can have trouble closing sales, trouble saying, "How many can I put you down for?" He hesitates to offend by becoming too specific. He hesitates to risk his connection by having the customer say no.

In the end, Alex's world is about connection. Alex has moved around a great deal, and he has always prided himself on his adaptability and his ability to move right in and be at home, but he also needs a stable base. This means participating in some community, being part of something larger and more enduring than the moment. His concern for values expresses this need for stability in this quickly moving world, but he also expresses this need in his memberships. His activities in his town, in his church, and in his workplace all reflect this quest. Alex's sense of unity means that the organizations and institutions that he is part of, his memberships, become part of his identity, his sense of himself. Alex needs to see these organizations as worthy of his commitment and his role in these organizations as meaningful. Alex's sense of himself rests in his sense of connection. Until Alex found worthwhile connections, he was always lonely, despite his hundreds of friends.

Alex has made many good choices. He has found a job that challenges and rewards his gift for connecting and engaging, a job that gives him the variety and the stimulation that he needs, while also giving him the stability and the opportunities of a large organization, with its built-in networks and linkages. He feels good about his organization; these are good people doing good work. This has been a good world for him. He's also learned that he needs to build similar stimulating but stable bases in his family and his community. He's learned to accept his moments of frantic chaos as part of the price of being himself. He can laugh at his moments of frenzy. He knows who he is, and he knows what he is part of. He feels good about his life.

10

The DFT Pattern

DFTs see a world of options and priorities, with little objective constraint. They see a world of possibilities and opportunities. DFTs are explorers, adventurers, and entrepreneurs.

Karen is a DFT who is a partner in a new consulting group that specializes in data base design in distributed systems. She has promised her father that someday she will explain what that means. She and her partners Martin and Chris are meeting in an airport club between flights in different directions. Chris is saying, "This is an important deal for us. This is one of the top ten banks in the country, they'll pay top dollar, and it's big enough to keep us busy for at least a year. We need the money, guys. This would be a life saver."

Chris and Martin begin to talk numbers and resources while Karen stares out the window at the rain on the runways. "The money's good," she says suddenly, "but the deal feels wrong. I don't like it. Come on, these kinds of portfolio conversions are why we left the bank in the first place. Been there, done that." Her voice picks up speed as she talks. "We can do it, of course. Bring in some temps and all that. But it's wrong. This isn't the kind of client we want or the kind of work we want. It's going to pull us away from what we're trying to build. If it's a matter of survival, sure, but I don't see it." She stops and gazes at the other two.

Chris says, "Karen, we're in business to make money, and this is good money."

Karen shakes her head vigorously and leans forward, "I just don't see it. Maybe it's the smart move. It's sure the safe move. But it isn't taking us anywhere, it isn't going to stretch us, it isn't going to take us where we want to go."

They speak back and forth for a while and then Karen stands up. "We're getting nowhere, and I've got a flight. Let's conference tonight. That will give each of us a chance to think about what we want to do with this business. Let's see what our options are."

* * * * *

As a DFT, Karen sees a world of options, opportunities, and risks, a world of possibilities. She sees life as a constant challenge, like rafting white-water rapids. You react quickly and instinctively, making it up as you go along, improvising. This world is exciting, fast, and turbulent. Karen laughs when people talk about three-year plans. Who knows what the world is going to look like in three years? Who knows what it's going to look like next week? That's what makes it interesting. What keeps her on course is her sense of the possibilities, the sharp images she carries of where she wants to go. When people talk of her "vision," Karen rolls her eyes, but it is still true. She sees the chaos as exciting because she sees where she is going. The possibilities seem so clear. Possibility, direction, and vision are so central to her sense of the world that she cannot imagine that others don't see them as clearly as she does.

Karen is unimpressed by talk of careful processes and sound procedures. She imagines that these might be useful for other people, but her instinctive response is to start complaining about bureaucracy. "Why do you want to complicate things?" she'll ask, "just figure out what's important and do it. Don't get bogged down in all this little stuff." Being a middle manager in a large corporation was an endless trial for her. She felt like she was running through quicksand. She likes to claim that corporate life was an endless round of meetings, forms, and people telling her what she couldn't do. She learned many good lessons about the values of planning and the complexities of organizational dynamics, but the price was high. She learned to respect the uses of processes and procedures, the values of spreadsheets and Gantt charts, but she was also relieved to get out and start her own business.

Karen is an explorer and an adventurer. She responds quickly and happily to possibilities, to surprises, and to the unexpected. She likes not being certain what's going to happen tomorrow. We've described DFTs in earlier chapters as adventurous, urgent, outspoken, impulsive, persuasive, impromptu, bold, and ad hoc, but remember that the key is Karen's perception, not her action: how her world looks, not simply what she does. Karen improvises and takes risks because that style makes sense in the world she sees. Her world does not look routine or predictable. Motion, not stability, is the key to her world. Defining, predicting, or controlling seem pointless, like taking compass readings in a hurricane. This world has shape and coherence not because of what it is but because of what it is becoming. Only a sense of the future gives shape to the present. Sometimes the future seems more real to Karen than the events that actually surround her. The possibilities excite her.

Predicting, analyzing, and planning don't count for much in this shifting world. There's a wonderful story about an American regimental commander in World War II, just before the invasion of France, speaking to his regiment. He held up the phone-book size official plan for the regiment's assault on a Normandy beach, tossed it over his shoulder, and said, "There's nothing in this plan that's going to go right. Just get yourself onto the beach, and I'll tell you what to do." This would be Karen's approach. She wouldn't doubt that she would know what to do. She trusts her "radar" as she calls it, her sense of the right direction.

"Don't get bogged down in the small stuff" is both her strength and her weakness. Her weakness is her distaste for detail, structure, and analysis. She bores easily and finds boredom intolerable. Remember that she doesn't see much objective structure or detail in her world. She sees possibilities better than she sees facts. She's smart and she can read a spreadsheet, but she doesn't find much inspiration there. The reality and importance of detail is an abstraction for her, not a matter of immediate gut experience. She leads project teams that do detailed work, but she sees her job as keeping people moving in the right direction and responding to the inevitable crises. She lets others do the details. When she hears the story about the Normandy invasion, she knows that someone had to arrange for thousands of ships to cross the English Channel to put soldiers on the beach, but she's glad it wasn't her. This "small stuff" doesn't grab her.

Karen's greatest talents are her sense of direction, her sense of what is important and what is unimportant, her sense of possibility, and her willingness to take risks because she sees payoffs. This is the strategic sense of the DFT. You wouldn't turn to Karen for strategic planning, because she doesn't plan, but you would turn to her to see if you are moving in the right direction, if you are seeing the possibilities as well as the risks. She doesn't plan in any conventional sense. She doesn't create a series of steps; she doesn't set objectives or concrete goals. She has trouble appreciating the impersonal and the objective, the very elements on which good plans rest. She shops without lists, and she long ago gave up trying to use coupons. So she spends a little more than she might and sometimes she ends up with eighteen rolls of paper towels and no dishwasher soap, but that is a small price to pay to avoid making lists and tracking coupons. Detailed plans, maps, and programs irritate Karen, because she knows she is going to have to improvise at key points, regardless of the plan.

These plans seem like wasted energy and pointless complexity. Karen sees where she wants to be and is frustrated by people who want to focus on the details of the terrain between here and there.

Of course, sometimes she misses the point completely. She isn't a magician, and her sense of direction, her sense of vision, isn't always right. She can trip over details that she didn't notice. She can misjudge the terrain. She can be brilliantly right or ignominiously wrong, but she always enjoys rolling the dice. Karen has learned to look at the numbers, to respect the details and the evidence, to check that she is going the right way, but the numbers will never decide for her. If she's wrong, she's wrong. Mistakes can be fixed, and being wrong is just another way of learning.

Remember that Karen do not "make" decisions. She *sees* decisions, choices, and options. This is not an intellectual, rational process. Learning to *make* decisions, particularly factual decisions, has been difficult for Karen. When she was deciding to leave her employer to set up her own company, her husband helped her review their finances, create cash flow estimates, and list the advantages and disadvantages of this move. In truth, she did this simply to make him happy. She knew starting her own company was the right thing to do. If the numbers had shown this to be foolish, she would have accepted that with reluctance. She's learned to allow the evidence to say "no," but she is the one who has to say "yes." She is uncomfortable with decisions that are "arrived at" by some logical process. The decisions that she trusts are those that simply appear.

In Karen's world, you have to trust your instincts. If the numbers agree with you, so much the better. Karen's great talent is seeing through complexities and details to what is most important — "get on the beach and I'll tell you what to do" — and then doing whatever will take her there. Her sense of possibility is so sharp that she is willing to take the risks that will get her there. Risk is part of the game, a test of your confidence in what you see. Risk is always personal for Karen, not a matter of actuarial tables and statistics. Most start-up businesses fail, she knows, but those numbers, she thinks, simply don't apply to her. They may apply to the world in general, but not to her. The limits and constraints imposed by the impersonal and objective facts are very small in her world. Obstacles don't look very big. She trusts her radar. She's learned that she's more willing to roll the dice, to take a chance, than most people. She's not sure why this is; she doesn't think of herself as especially courageous. Perhaps she just sees something that others don't.

People see Karen as intense, bold, and stimulating, or as reckless, arrogant, and unpredictable. All of these can be true. At her best and at her worst, Karen is intense and wholehearted. She doesn't do things halfway. When something or someone catches her interest, that becomes her focus and she is wholly engaged. Many things can catch her interest and engage her imagination, at least briefly. Her enthusiasm when she first engages a task or idea or relationship, however, is balanced by her loss of interest when the territory becomes too familiar. Karen is a better starter than finisher. Attention span, sadly, is not one of Karen's glories, but she has learned to trust her energy. When something interests her, she acts; when it stops interesting her, she stops. When she is not wholly absorbed, her attention wanders until she finds something that does absorb her. This confuses and angers people who want her to act more predictably. They complain that she is thoughtless, fickle, inattentive, and distractible, descriptions that do fit immature or highly stressed DFTs. Karen is not thoughtless; she is, however, often restless. Karen often finds herself restless and bored, needing to move, needing to do something different, something new. Restlessness is one of her most familiar feelings; it almost seems like an old friend.

Karen has learned to master her restlessness by focusing on tasks, projects, concerns, and relationships that she finds absorbing and exciting. Everything else must go into second place. She needs a sense of vocation or mission, a sense that what she is doing matters and makes a difference. Without this sense in key parts of her life, Karen would flounder. Her restless could become destructive. Even when she is working from a strong sense of direction, some people see her as a troublemaker or instigator because she enjoys stirring things up. Her restlessness can be a trial for both Karen and for others, but she is rarely boring.

Karen wants constant changes, opportunities, and possibilities. She grows restless if asked to repeat old formulas or follow in others' footsteps. She moved through a rapid succession of positions in her corporate life, moving on as soon as she felt she had gotten the feel for the position and had made a mark. Karen wants movement and visible impact. Once she's made an impact, she's ready to go. When things become routine, Karen creates ways to keep herself interested, introducing new ideas or processes to keep her interest engaged. Although Karen is not always aware of this, she loves to have impact, to make a difference, and to leave a mark. In a world of possibilities, turning possibilities into realities is exciting. Making things happen and having an effect test how clearly you see, and Karen values this deeply. She is uncomfortable is settings that are so stable, large, or routine that she cannot make a difference.

Karen prides herself on her readiness to move forward, to go ahead, but like all people, Karen brings both strengths and vulnerabilities to her actions. Her strengths include her fascination with the new and unknown, her willingness to improvise and experiment, her willingness to make guesses and take risks, her willingness to change plans quickly, and her willingness to drop approaches that aren't working. These strengths are also her weaknesses, because Karen avoids preparing, rehearsing, maintenance, and routine logistics. Her partners like to rehearse before presenting reports to clients, for example, but Karen feels she does better without rehearsing, that she brings freshness and energy that she would lose by too much preparation. Sometimes this is true; sometimes it is not. She tries to be sensitive to the risks she takes in these areas, but she feels she has to do what works best for her. She is impatient with preparation and rehearsal because they feel lifeless. Rehearsing a sales pitch or a presentation doesn't engage Karen. She relies on the adrenaline of the moment, rather than careful preparation, to drive her performances. Learning to accept the necessity and desirability of these "boring" tasks, however, is a key growth point for Karen.

Preparation, planning, and routine are uncomfortable for Karen, but she makes a mistake when she falls into disdain and contempt for these practices. Her disdain can become one of the greatest sources of stress in her life. When Karen ignores the demands of facts, logic, and organization, she creates chaos that can overwhelm her. "I've found my keys," she'll say, "now where's my car?" Under stress, Karen becomes more restless, more unsettled, hopping from task to task, starting things she never finishes, dropping a task midway and starting another, creating more and more disorder around her. The smart move for Karen is to stop, to take a deep breath, and to write a plan of action. This is difficult, because she wants to move not to plan, but planning is good because it creates a sense of order. She has also found that routine tasks can be soothing when she is under stress: bringing her expense accounts current, paying some bills, cleaning her desk. She always has to force herself to start these tasks, but somehow they help. The chaos feels less overwhelming. She also needs occasionally to just do nothing, although this is probably impossible when she is feeling stressed. She lives with an inner voice that is constantly demanding, "hurry up; don't just stand around looking at your feet; opportunity never knocks twice; do something, do anything." She needs to learn to stand still sometimes, to consider patiently the possibilities without leaping into action. She also needs to understand that this will never be her strength. Moving, not standing, is her strength; even on vacations, she will be much happier in motion than trying to sit still.

While action is the arena to which we most readily attach words like "adventure" or "risk," Karen brings similar strengths and vulnerabilities into the realms of ideas and relationships. Karen has strong artistic and intellectual passions, for example. She loves both jazz and 19th century novels, and she brings her adventurous approach to these enthusiasms. She loves to find new works and to immerse herself. She loves to talk about what she's hearing or reading. She loves to argue positions and will jump from position to position for the sheer joy of it. She's not a great scholar or expert because she won't read or listen to the boring stuff, and her knowledge is unsystematic and filled with gaps. She compensates with simple audacity, generalizing boldly, inventing examples, and deducing possibilities. She laughs and says that everyone thinks you know what you're talking about if you say it fast and with gusto. Knowledge is difficult, she says, but opinions are easy.

Karen is an action learner, learning by immersion, by trial-and-error, by hands-on experience. Listening to someone present information, for example, doesn't help her. She needs to talk; she needs to have dialogue; she needs to argue. She learns better by speaking and writing than by listening and reading. She learns by acting, by doing. Reflecting afterwards is very valuable to her – although this is a discipline she has had to work to acquire. She's learned to reflect on her successes and failures, rather than immediately moving ahead, and she's found this very useful. One of Karen's great strengths in learning is that she doesn't fear mistakes. She knows that learning to walk means falling down and getting up. She doesn't worry about looking foolish or silly if she can see that she is moving forward. When she's in Paris, she enjoys speaking her bad French. If you're not willing to make mistakes, you can't learn. If you aren't willing to fall, you will crawl forever.

Karen handles information by skimming and dipping. She'll move rapidly through a large amount of information until she sees something that intrigues her, which she will grab from the mass and then keep moving. She often reads just the first chapter and last chapter of books or just the introduction to articles. That's where she finds most of the good stuff. With some experience, learning from mistakes and false grabs, Karen has become skilled at this approach, quickly finding the key piece on which everything else rests. She works well with incomplete and partial information, and she responds quickly because she isn't slowed by details. Karen is not learning details or facts, although inevitably, some details and facts will stick. She is learning what is important, what is central, what is key. Perhaps because she ignores so much detail, Karen is learning to create a coherent picture from a few strokes. She loves to create slogans and brief headlines that capture her understanding. These are like those drawings that use a few bold lines to catch the essence of a figure or a face or a landscape.

Karen is quick and innovative with ideas. Her partners call her "the creative one" because she isn't bound by how things have been done before. When complimented for "seeing outside the box," she'll say that she didn't realize there was a box. Creativity takes many forms, but Karen's creativity lies in improvising, experimenting, and taking risks. She improvises with ideas as well as she improvises with actions. She enjoys novelty. If you look about, you'll see people like Karen in places like creative marketing, strategic planning, and product design, as well as in management and in their own businesses.

This same sense of possibility and creativity mark Karen's social life and relationships. People are attracted by her energy, confidence, and intensity, and then puzzled, irritated, or angered by the problem of how to hold her attention. One moment she seems completely focused and absorbed in the other person, and the next moment she is simply gone. Karen does little to build and maintain relationships. She is as casual with the "small stuff" and the routine in her relationships as she is in her work. She cares most about the relationships where she feels an immediate and strong bond to the other person, a sense of personal connection that survives neglect, geographic distance, and the passing of time. Her central relationships, whether with mentors, friends, or lovers, need to challenge her, to be unpredictable and exciting, and to hold the possibility of surprise and perhaps the edge of danger. This, in turn, is what she offers in return. She offers excitement, not predictability. These people are the center of her life, and she has found them in odd places. Her husband, one of her partners, her best friend from childhood, and a couple of old teachers are here, but so is her hairdresser, an ex-boyfriend, and the cleaning woman at her office. She feels intense loyalty to these people. Other people are less significant. She likes them and enjoys them, but she doesn't make much effort to be with them. When people realize this, they can be hurt. When people ask her to be predictable, they will be disappointed.

Karen can seem abrupt and intolerant. She is impatient with the slower paces of other people and pushes them to move more quickly. Sometimes she realizes that she is tapping her foot to try to get someone to speak more quickly. She has had to struggle with her urge to finish people's sentences for them. Patience is an unending struggle for her. Her friends laugh at stories of how she has abandoned full grocery carts at the store because the checkout line was too long. Her sense of urgency, time pressure, and need to move ahead can be a strength, but it also leads to careless errors, inefficiencies, and superficiality. At work, Karen has trouble waiting for people to catch up with her and allowing people to seek the information or sense of connection they need before they can move ahead. People have the sense of Karen pacing restlessly, impatiently, irritably, and this has the paradoxical effect of making it harder for them to move ahead. Presenting a report to her can be frightening. Karen can immobilize people with her impatience.

Listening patiently is difficult for her. She wants to listen just long enough to get a sense of what the other is saying and then respond. Remember that Karen learns by doing. Karen doesn't learn by listening; she learns by talking. Karen loves to argue, though perhaps we should more politely say that she loves to engage in dialogue. People sometimes see this as controlling and dominating, but this is a mistake. Karen does sometimes control and dominate, but arguing and discussing is how she tries to understand. She expects others to do the same, to persuade and push back. She knows by experience that people often don't push back, but she can't understand why. In a room full of people like Karen, you will routinely hear each one talking simultaneously and talking loudly to be heard over the uproar. This horrifies other people, but Karen enjoys the energy of the room and sees nothing odd about it. Karen needs to talk so that she knows what she is thinking.

All Karen's communication is persuasive. She wants you to see things as she does. "This is good," she is saying, "believe it and act on it." She wants movement. Her confidence, her certainty, and her commitment are the heart of her persuasiveness. Karen speaks confidently and influentially. She draws people into her passions. Passion and enthusiasm are the center of her communication and influence. Content is secondary. This is one reason that preparation and rehearsal seem stilted and unreal to her; the engagement and absorption of the moment energizes her, and she relies on impromptu, improvised, ad hoc communications, rather than planned, rehearsed, or canned material. Sometimes this serves her brilliantly. Other times, this strategy leaves her floundering and rambling. People see her as good at selling, but she sells because she believes.

Karen's communication can be both urgent and vague. When she gives orders at work, for example, it is likely to be something like, "Well, you'll have to do better than that," or "This isn't going to work; fix it." She points at the target, but she doesn't say much about what you are supposed to do. She doesn't tell you how to do better or how to fix it. People nod, walk away, and come back later with questions. Karen thinks she is doing well: she knows that she doesn't want people telling her how to do things; she knows that she has no interest in step by step instructions. Other people, however, may want more content.

In both her social life and her work life, Karen shows a cycle of engaging and withdrawing. She engages when she is interested and curious and withdraws when she is bored. She engages to have influence and impact and withdraws when impact is not possible. In groups she cannot dominate, influence, and shape, Karen pulls back and says little. Her silence marks either her frustration or her lack of interest. She participates in teams more to make things happen than to enjoy the interactions. She wants her teams to move, to go somewhere, to do something. The roles she is happiest playing include energizer, advocate, and confronter, as she pushes the team ahead. The norms she imposes on a team, the standards she uses to evaluate a team, are "be adventurous," "be creative," and "don't hesitate." In a key sense, Karen is not a "good team player." She sets her own course and chooses her own direction, and she is not ordinarily interested in any group's input or influence. She goes her own way.

These cycles of engagement and disengagement are major features of Karen's life. She is a sprinter, not a distance runner. When Karen is engaged and absorbed, she goes until she drops from exhaustion. There's no "slow and steady wins the race" here. You sprint, then you collapse. People assume that Karen has limitless energy, but this isn't so. She looks so energetic because of her enthusiasm. When she is bored, her energy dissipates quickly. Karen beats herself up for this periodically. She wishes she had more perseverance and endurance. She's learned, however, to trust her energy. She goes when she's ready, and she stops when she's ready.

The best environments – the best work, relationships, and recreations – for Karen are those that allow her to explore, to try new things, to seek adventures. Karen does not thrive in environments that demand patience, routine, carefully honed skills, thoughtful analysis, and careful nurture. Karen has learned to respect these processes, but she should never put herself in positions where these processes become central to her success and happiness. If she does, she will fail.

11

The DTF Pattern

DTFs see a world of options and judgments, a world of clearly defined goals, with limited context. They see a world a world of simple choices with simple consequences. They are warriors, battlers, and figures of authority.

Charles is a DTF who runs Human Resources for one business unit of a Fortune 500 company. He's just met with the head of the business unit and now he's meeting with four of his direct reports. He is saying, "What I'm going to say has to stay inside this room. We're going to do some contingency planning, and I don't want this on the grapevine. Is that understood?" He pauses, looking directly at each of his people as they nod their heads and murmur their agreement. "Okay. We're looking at some major reorganization. You know what our numbers have looked like, so you knew this could be coming. Dan wants a plan for cutting $10,000,000 from our personnel budget, and he wants that plan in 48 hours. I hope you can rearrange your schedules to give me those 48 hours." He smiles briefly; of course they will rearrange their schedules.

"Fine," he resumes, "now talk to me. An hour from now I want the issues identified and I want assignments made. What are we looking at?" He leans back, folding his hands behind his head, and waits. His people look at each other silently for a moment. They know they're not here to discuss the wisdom of layoffs; they're here to decide the mechanics. They begin talking while Charles listens and watches. They discuss the number of positions they'll need to cut. They discuss how to select people for displacement. They discuss the contents and costs of separation packages and outplacement services. They discuss communication issues both within the unit and in the community. They make lists on flip charts, while Charles sits and listens, asking an occasional question.

After 45 minutes, he interrupts. "Have we hit the major issues?" he asks. They agree that they have. "I think so, too," Charles says. "Fine. So let's make some assignments. Most of them are obvious, but let's get them on paper. Karen," he says, looking to his communications specialist, "I want you to take responsibility for getting this plan together. This thing's going to be a mess, and I want good spin. I want to see all of you and a preliminary plan at 9:00 tomorrow morning. Any problems?" He looks around and his people tell him they're ready. "Okay, let's do it. I'll be available. And remember — no rumors, no gossip. I'll see you tomorrow."

* * * * *

As a DTF, Charles sees a world of clear, simple options, with little ambiguity and little gray. "Challenges" is a word he likes, because it captures his sense of the world — he sees a world of challenges. He sees right and wrong, good and bad, smart and stupid, loyal and disloyal. He sees a world of sharp edges, a world that combines possibilities with facts to create goals and opportunities. Challenges and goals are the most important features of his world, and he organizes and directs his life around them. The facts either serve or resist these possibilities, building the objective framework of resources and obstacles through which he moves. This is a world of yes or no. "You're either on the bus or you're not on the bus," Charles likes to say.

Charles is puzzled and irritated when people talk about the complexity of problems, about shadings and nuances. He thinks people are simply looking for reasons not to take responsibility and reasons not to act. The world is difficult, but it is not complicated – you look for the biggest challenge and you take it on. People make things too complicated, he thinks. The direct way is usually the best way. You don't want to leap without looking, but you also don't want to sit around talking about the difficulties of leaping. Charles is puzzled by what he sees as the persistent irresponsibility of people. People seem not to see the challenges, and they busy themselves with politics and irrelevant distractions rather than face what is in front of them. He understands that the choices are not always appealing, but that doesn't justify not choosing.

The options and possibilities that Charles sees are clear-cut. You face one challenge, deal with it, and move on to the next. You don't try to plan seven challenges in advance. That's needless and immobilizing complexity. You deal with what's in front of you and worry about the consequences only if they become problems. You cross bridges when you get to them. Right now, the challenge Charles sees is cutting costs to keep earnings up. He knows that if they fail there, the parent company may well dump his business unit. That is the problem now. He also knows that sharp staff cuts will have consequences down the road, but there's no point in worrying about that yet. First things first. In essence, Charles looks at the world and asks, "Which challenge matters most *now* and how can I meet that challenge?"

DTF is a forceful pattern, describing people like Charles who are intensely focused, disciplined, and driving. This is the pattern that American business has most admired and idealized, because it is results-driven and competitive. Our stereotypes of the hard-driving businessperson, however, don't do justice to the complexity and humanity of people like Charles, nor do they do justice to the limits and vulnerabilities of this style. We've already characterized Charles as determined, demanding, focused, assured, disciplined, forceful, and directive, but now we need to try to understand how he sees the world, and how the world he sees leads him to act as he does.

Charles sees challenges, opportunities, resources, and obstacles. He sees battles that he is determined to win. His world is exciting, but it has a dark tinge, an edge of danger. "Here be dragons," his maps say, "Here be enemy." Charles sees the impending lay-offs, for example, as a challenge and a battle. His first responsibility is to spot the dangers, the obstacles, and the problems, so that they can be overcome. This is a risky world, and only the strong and the prepared succeed. You identify obstacles so you can prepare to overcome them. Charles spends much time focused on dangers, obstacles, and what can go wrong. Being responsible means being prepared. You don't act impulsively, but you also never back away. In this embattled world, Charles values both strength and responsibility, the warrior's virtues. His single-mindedness creates enormous momentum as he moves forward, so that he is difficult to either stop or divert, like a locomotive moving down a track. Strength, focus, preparation and determination are the tools with which he negotiates his life, while responsibility – whom and what he takes care of – gives meaning and depth to his life.

The concept of responsibility is central to Charles. He seeks responsibility and he accepts responsibility. In the current crisis, for example, Charles feels a strong loyalty and responsibility to the leadership team and the stockholders, so he will execute the lay-offs efficiently. But he also feels a responsibility to the employees, so he will also execute the lay-offs fairly and quickly. He believes that dragging these things out, letting rumors outstrip facts and anxieties mount, is both irresponsible and unkind. He won't let that happen. He takes his responsibilities seriously, and he expects others to do the same.

Charles' great strength is the sharp focus with which he attacks problems and difficulties, mapping a path to follow and unhesitatingly following that path. Charles is goal-driven. This phrase has become cliched, but Charles is not interested in slogans or posters. His goals give shape and focus to his world, and he cannot imagine moving through the day without goals. Goals clarify his world. His running is a great example. He had run for exercise with little enthusiasm for several years. It was simply something he thought he should do, so he did it. Then one day, he decided to train for a marathon. Suddenly, running became interesting. He created a program and he stuck to it. He could chart his progress. He had a sense that he was *doing* something, not simply going out for a jog. Now every year, he selects one marathon and trains for it.

He loves having a goal. Sometimes he writes his goals down; more often he simply knows them. He cannot imagine that others may not focus on goals as he does. He sets goals in his personal life as well as in his business life. After a rough patch in his marriage a couple of years ago, for example, he began to set goals of spending certain amounts of time alone with his wife and identifying activities they could share. He tries to call her from work at least once a day, because he knows that pleases her. He's found that this works for him. Goals are markers; you can measure your progress toward the goal; you can know how you are doing. Situations where he has no goals are uncomfortable for him, because he doesn't know what to do or how he is doing. He has learned from bitter experience that he cannot simply sit on a beach. He needs a goal. He has found that even the chitchat at the beginning of meetings is endurable if he sets a goal, even if it's only to get Marcy from the CFO's office to smile.

His focus is also Charles' great weakness, because his focus can blind him. He dislikes interruptions and diversions and will often sit blankly through discussions that feel irrelevant to him, desperate to return to real work. His focus can be so intense that he doesn't notice other people, other choices, or other. His wife jokes that he is like a thoroughbred racehorse, wearing blinders so he can only see the finish line. When he has planned a picnic, he expects to go on the picnic, even if it is raining. When his running schedule calls for him to run eight miles, he runs eight miles, even if he has had an exhausting day.

Charles has always remembered vividly his first management job, because he failed. He tried to drive up sales in a small retail branch by setting goals and driving his staff as he would drive himself. Chaos followed. People quit; people complained to the regional manager; people found dozens of excuses for not following his instructions. Fortunately, he had a good regional manager who helped him see his mistakes, helped him see that he needed to take account of people's assorted loyalties, friendships, and commitments, helped him see that he had to involve people and win their trust and commitment. He's learned the lesson, though he still resents having to waste time on these issues. He was terribly hurt, however, that his employees saw him as an insensitive and uncaring tyrant, because he knew how much he cared. He was trying to help them succeed, but they didn't understand that.

Charles has grown and matured in recognizing that the world is not always as simple as it seems. There are landmines and booby traps, and he's learned that his tight focus can blind him to these hidden issues. His impulse is to label all this complexity "politics" and to scorn it, but he's found that that is self-defeating. Now he steps back and looks around occasionally, to see what he's missing. He knows that downsizing is a rational and inevitable response to the company's current problems, for example, but he has learned that people will respond emotionally to any plans he makes and will probably blame him. When he was younger, he would have simply dismissed these reactions as "stupid." Now he tries to anticipate them and take them into account.

Charles radiates authority. His focus, certainty, and calm give him great influence. People look to him when they feel unsure. They know that he will accept responsibility. He looks confident, he looks focused, and he looks like he knows what he's doing, even when he's unsure. Charles doesn't wait until he is certain before he acts; he believes that certainty will come from acting. His willingness to act and to take responsibility gives him influence and authority. Sometimes Charles tires of always being the responsible one, the one who breaks up the party and sends people back to work, but he also cannot ignore the responsibilities that are so clear. Charles inspires respect, and he values and seeks this respect from others, but he sometimes misses the affection and warmth. There is a core of loneliness in most DTFs. Responsibility is difficult.

Charles demands much of himself and of others. He values self-discipline and he distrusts emotionality. You don't succeed by having fun; you succeed by working hard. He has created a careful structure for his life, a structure that takes him toward his goals and that he can monitor and evaluate. He arises early and gets to work early. He works from lists and schedules and monitors his progress through the day by checking items off his lists. He has a fixed time in the late afternoon when he exercises, and he uses that to punctuate his day. He devotes his evenings to his family and refuses to allow work to intrude on this time. He likes structure and order in his life. The routine can be a refuge, a place of sanctuary, away from the battles. He may wear the same clothes, drive the same car, and keep the same social activities indefinitely. This keeps things simple, so he can focus on what really matters. His structure and routine free him to focus.

Charles uses external goals and objectives to tell him how he is doing. He wants visible markers showing that he is making progress on his chosen path, and he wants the satisfaction of seeing what he has done. Charles is a runner who sets mileage goals. When he was in sales, he set his own quotas; even from his current staff position, he pays strict attention to his company's return-on-equity and stock-value goals. His office wall is covered with charts and graphs. He likes to see how he is doing. This is his planning. It is simple, uncomplicated, and to the point. "This is what I want, and this is how I know I'm on the right road." Charles focuses on practical, short-term objectives, rather than vague, grandiose visions that are difficult to evaluate. Attempting the impossible rarely appeals to Charles. The unattainable and the unmeasurable bore him.

Charles is strong in emergencies, which call upon his best gifts. Where others are uncertain, Charles moves straight ahead. He doesn't do tantrums, hysterics, outbursts, or panic. He is task-centered and solution-centered. In his intensity, however, Charles can ignore others and lose perspective. He has trouble with the emotional side of crises. He sees emotional displays as simply distracting and irrelevant, but his own usual calm and certainty can slip into teeth-gritting, humorless obsession. Charles is relentless, in both the best and the worst senses of that word. When frustrated in pursuing a goal, Charles simply pushes harder and becomes more focused. He has difficulty monitoring himself, so he doesn't notice when he is becoming fatigued or ill or emotional. When someone else points out that he is acting angry or sad or tired, he is often caught by surprise. He doesn't like looking inside; the psyche is not to be understood; it is to be disciplined and mastered. No touchy-feely for him. He is a hunch player with little curiosity about the sources of his hunches. As a salesperson, for example, he called on the same unresponsive customer for years, convinced that the next call would be the one that sells, and perhaps it will be, but then again perhaps it won't. "Refuse to lose" is Charles' motto, but learning to reevaluate goals and change approaches is his challenge. Charles has trouble dropping goals and changing plans in midstream. Dropping a goal feels like a defeat, not like a choice.

Charles responds to stress by trying harder and by doing more and more by himself. He withdraws into his office and tries to do everything, while being angry that no one is helping him. One of the hardest lessons in his life has been to learn to ask for help. He hates that, because admitting he can't do something feels like weakness and failure. He's learning that people like to be asked to help, that people feel more comfortable with him when he can admit occasional weakness, but this is still difficult.

Charles learns best when he has access to clear, well-structured, well-organized, and unadorned information. He loves summaries, outlines, and bullet points. The key questions for him are "What do I need to know here? How is this going to take me where I want to go?" He likes to ask questions, so he learns better from presentations and discussions than from reading, but he has little interest in group interactions. He wants to discuss with the experts, not with people who know less than he does. He wants to be informed and persuaded, not entertained and amused.

Charles is an excellent listener, and listening is his favorite way to get information because he can push the speaker to summarize and then he can question where he is not clear. He listens actively – he asks questions, he asks for summaries, and he gives immediate reactions. This style intimidates people who don't know what they're talking about or people who are just trying to convey an impression, because it reveals quickly that they don't have much content. Charles listens for content, and he has little patience for rambling and pointless discussion. He isn't concerned with the personal or social context. He used to become quite irritated when people would stop by his cubicle, look in, and say, "What are you doing?" "What does it look like I'm doing? I'm working," he would snap back. It never occurred to him that these people were simply trying to back a connection to him.

Charles sees himself as hardheaded, pragmatic, and by-the-numbers, but in truth he is highly intuitive and selective. He forms opinions quickly and abandons them slowly. He gathers data to support his opinions and conclusions and ignores data that challenges his opinions. This keeps his focus tight but poses obvious risks. Charles respects facts and logic, but his great talent is sifting data. He sorts information quickly into two stacks: a small stack of information that is relevant to his current challenges, a stack he will use, and a larger stack that seems irrelevant, a stack he will ignore. Charles has a genius for tuning out "irrelevant" information. This is both useful and dangerous, and Charles does make mistakes by ignoring information that seems peripheral or unimportant but that comes back to hurt him. As Charles has matured and become more effective, he has learned to question himself and challenge his own opinions to limit this possible rigidity. He's good at changing his mind, but he requires some tough convincing.

People see Charles as pragmatic and focused, but he has varied and surprising interests. In the last couple of years, for instance, he has developed a great fondness for classic Japanese woodblock printings – *ukiyo-e* – and he spends a good bit of time on the internet checking auctions and sales. He has a nice collection of these prints, and this comes as a great surprise to people who come to his home for the first time. It seems so unlike him, and he never mentions it at work. Charles is more complicated than he looks. He looks simple because he keeps parts of himself private.

His focus can make social interactions uncomfortable for him. He wants his interactions to be direct, uncomplicated, task-centered and frank, and he feels both clumsy and bored at social pleasantries and other unfocused interactions. He can be brusque and abrupt in dealing with people. Even with the people whom he cares most about, the people he is most intimate with, there is always a little distance, a little coolness. It has never occurred to him, for example, to discuss his interest in Japanese art with his co-workers. Why would he do that? What is the point here? The idea of simply spending time with people to express affection or care or to build alliances or bonds is difficult for Charles to accept.

This does not imply that Charles is cold and uncaring. This is an unfair caricature. In his role in human resources, for example, Charles has had to fire a number of people. He finds this painful, but he neither complains about it nor commiserates with the people he is firing. Telling them how difficult this is for him would be unfair, he thinks. He tries to be direct, objective, and business-like, and this leads many people to think he is undisturbed and uncaring. Quite the contrary, Charles cares intensely, but his caring can be hard to read. He believes caring is better expressed in actions than in words, and he underestimates people's need to hear the words that go with the actions. Talking about these things is difficult for Charles. He believes his actions should speak for him, but he needs to understand that people don't always understand actions without words. He also needs to learn that others can express this same caring and passion in other ways.

Charles doesn't do subtle. He is direct and blunt in his approach to others and that is what he wants in return. He doesn't read hidden agendas, deeper layers of meaning, or subtle hints well. He likes interactions direct and spelled out, and he thinks his own actions reflect this. He says what's on his mind, and he doesn't concern himself with how this appears to others. He wants to focus on content and tasks, not people's feelings and personal agendas. Trying to make sense of these subjective dimensions of human relationships exhausts him. "Why," he complains to his friends, "can't people just say what they mean? Why can't they just spit it out?"

Conflict and disagreement don't disturb Charles. He sees conflict as useful. He likes to see the issues on the table, and he likes to deal with them directly. Charles is direct and forceful in expressing his views, but he also listens well when others respond in the same way. He likes to argue, but he intensely dislikes evasion, sugarcoating, and hidden agendas. He doesn't respect anyone who won't fight with him. His meetings with his direct reports can get pretty loud, but he enforces strict norms about not getting personal and sticking to the topic. He wants conflicts focused so they can be resolved. His friends and employees are endlessly surprised when he stops in what seems the middle of an argument and says "You're right," and the discussion is over.

Charles prefers dealing with people individually rather than in groups. He finds himself avoiding groups. He's not a joiner. He feels responsibility toward his community, for example, but he simply won't participate in any community work that requires that he sit in meetings. He already resents the amount of time he spends in meetings at work, and he's not about to volunteer for more. He simply doesn't see meetings as useful ways to accomplish anything. There's too much talk and too little action. Too much is going on that is too hard to follow, too many crosscurrents, alliances, enmities, and hidden agendas. Charles responds either by withdrawing or by attempting to dominate the group. He is more comfortable and flexible with individuals. He enjoys people, but he doesn't enjoy meetings.

Despite all this (or perhaps because of it), Charles is excellent at leading and managing people. At his best, Charles is clear and direct about how he see things and what he expects. People routinely say, "At least you know where you stand with Charles," and this is a great compliment. When Charles gives orders, he gives orders. He doesn't give detailed instructions, he doesn't solicit input or interaction, he doesn't give long explanations, and he doesn't ask for help. He gives orders – "I want a draft on my desk by 9." People may experience this as brusque or rude, but people are never in doubt about what he wants.

Charles' clarity and forthrightness give him authority, and people look to him for guidance. All Charles asks for is performance, and he is good at managing performance. He gives clear instructions and direction; he sets clear and measurable goals; he creates objective standards; and he is an excellent model of the performance he expects. He is an involved manager. He wants to know what his people are doing and what challenges they face. He is demanding, but he never demands the impossible. He also demands more of himself than of anyone else. People who work for him always describe him as fair, and this carries great weight. They know he evaluates by performance, not by personality, and they know he doesn't play favorites.

Charles is an excellent task manager, but he has more trouble managing the personal and social issues that occur on the job. He knows that he has to pay some attention to these issues, but he also feels that this is secondary and a distraction. He wishes people would leave their personal lives at home and just come to work in order to work. "Sometimes," he says, "I think I'm just an overpaid babysitter." He has trouble grasping that anything could take priority over the task, so he can seem insensitive to people's needs and feelings. When this is pointed out, he is surprised and sorry, but this is a lesson he must learn repeatedly. Of course, he treats himself the same way.

Charles responds with assurance to challenges, but he has more difficulty with routine. Routine is too safe, and safety somehow unnerves him. He cannot trust it. He needs an edge of danger to feel involved and to take things seriously. He isn't careless of danger; he takes it seriously and prepares for it. He is careless about safety; he gets bored and he gets careless. He's found that he does best in business if he changes jobs with some frequency, because he's at his best in mastering new challenges, but he gets bored and distracted with maintaining routine.

Charles has found that he does best in environments that let him focus on tasks and challenges and environments that don't press him too hard on the subjective and personal. He likes environments with clear structure and expectations, with clear lines of authority and clear individual responsibilities. He doesn't feel comfortable sharing responsibility with groups and teams, and he knows he does better as an individual contributor than as a team player. Most importantly, he needs constant challenges. He has made some good choices to end up in his current position, which draws so well on his strengths.

12

Seeing Your Best Paths

Knowing yourself means knowing where to focus — and where not to focus — your efforts. This requires a good image or map. You find your best path by knowing yourself, building on your strengths, exploring your possibilities, and protecting yourself from your weaknesses.

Some people read books like this just because they're curious. They like to read about themselves, to see themselves in a new mirror and in a different light. But many of us want more than descriptions; we also want prescriptions. "OK," we'll say, "so I'm a TFD. That's cool, but now what?" We want to do better, to work more productively, to deal with others more effectively and smoothly, and to live more satisfying lives. We wish to make better choices and walk better paths.

We believe that we're giving you a good map for your travels. The map we are giving you is a clearer image of yourself, and this clearer image can help you make better choices by marking the paths that lead where you wish to go. We can't tell you how to live your life, because we don't know the choices you face, the values you cherish, the resources you have, or the responsibilities you bear. We can give you a better mirror in which to see yourself, and we believe that pondering what you see in that mirror will help you choose your way more wisely.

Our minds work through images and metaphors, through mental pictures that allow us to summon up realities and explore possibilities. They are our maps of reality. Our best images illuminate our paths through the darkness. Maps are beautiful images in themselves. When you are new to some geography – a city, a business complex, a tropical jungle, or a legal jungle – you routinely become lost. You don't yet have a map in your mind. You may have a few direct routes you can travel, but if you leave these routes, you are in trouble. You know how to get from the east parking lot to your desk and from your desk to the cafeteria, but if you wander you are lost. With experience and a little help from people who know the terrain, you begin to form a richer map that lets you run by the mail room on your way to the cafeteria or find your way in from the west parking lot. As your map – your image of the space – becomes richer, you move more competently and more confidently. You even become willing to explore the north wing.

Our images of ourselves are maps as well, mapping our accomplishments, our possibilities, and our limitations. An accurate image of yourself is as important as an accurate map of any terrain. You are on a journey and the possibilities of becoming lost are many. The more clear your image of yourself is, the more clear your choices are as you approach twists in the road. We hope that we are helping you form a better map of yourself. Of course, you must enrich and deepen this map by including what is unique and special about you and about your world, but your picture must include your strengths, your possibilities, and your vulnerabilities if it is to guide you to success.

Our images of success

We want to add to your map of yourself a better sense of your possibilities, of the paths that might work for you. We want to give you a clearer image of success. Most of us, despite our daydreams and fantasies, underestimate our possibilities. We confuse our habits with our limits and stick to the paths we know well. We stop exploring. This is sad. We all have real limits and real weaknesses, but we also have real strengths and real possibilities.

We succeed and we thrive when we accept our challenges and explore our paths. We stagnate and fail when we refuse our challenges or walk other people's paths. Change and growth are part of the image we are trying to create with TDF. This image roots change in stability. We believe you have an unchanging core, and we believe that this core gives you the strength to meet your challenges and move ahead in your life. The images of change and growth that most of us carry are not helpful enough, because they map only parts of the reality. Remember the story of the ten blind people, each trying to describe an elephant after touching only one part – the trunk or the tusk or the ear or the tail or the leg? They described what they felt quite well, only they were not describing the elephant.

Different images of growth and success seem to reflect the T, D, and F faces of reality. The T image of change focuses on skills; the D image focuses on self-expression; and the F image focuses on the settings that shape us. The T image suggests that we change by learning *how* to act differently; the D image suggests we focus on *what* we want to achieve; and the F image focuses on *why* we should change, on the pushes and pulls of our worlds. Each of these images reflects an important piece of reality and each has value, but they are incomplete. Learning skills is important and acting skillfully is a joy, but you are not simply a collection of skills. Self-expression is important, but expressing yourself requires both skills and an understanding of your setting. Understanding the settings that influence you is important, but you still need to act skillfully and your choices of settings express something about you.

The image we favor is the image of talent. Developing a talent is the best form of self-expression, but it requires discipline and skill, and our settings shape how we can express our talents. We've used the example of music before, because it is so illuminating. No musician believes that her music is simply a set of skills, because she knows that it expresses something central about her. Yet her music is a set of skills, a set of skills honed by years of effort, and her choice of the instrument and the music she plays is shaped by the musical culture in which she came to maturity. All serious growth, we believe, is like this: a person striving to express her gifts skillfully in complex and often confusing settings.

This image tells us important things about our journey through life.

- First, it tells us that our journeys require discipline and courage. One popular image today is that growth comes when you "follow your joy." We agree, but only if it is understood that this never means "do what's easy." Doing what's easy produces only mediocrity, and there is no joy in mediocrity.

- Second, you cannot thrive in isolation. Your settings pose both possibilities and dangers to your talents. Musical talent thrives only in an environment that encourages talent, supports development, and rewards performance. A setting that is indifferent or hostile to music can crush talent.

- Finally, the image tells us that we need to understand our talents. You can send any child to piano lessons, but only a few will become pianists. Knowing our talents, however, is difficult. We are given so many images of success that we become confused. Perhaps I should be like Michael Jordan or perhaps I should be like Mother Teresa. We confuse the reality of our talents with the fantasies the world paints.

The image of success that we are sketching is both simple and paradoxical: you are who you are, and you cannot be anyone else. You succeed when you are yourself and when you use your natural talents and gifts in their best settings. You fail when you deny your real talents and possibilities. Success in our work, our families, our friendships, our communities, and our artistic and spiritual endeavors rests on realism. We must know who we are; we must know our strengths and our possibilities. We must also know who we are not: we must know our weaknesses and our limitations.

Looking at yourself honestly is difficult. We don't want to look at our flaws and limitations. Or perhaps we can only see our flaws and limits and cannot see our strengths and possibilities. Or perhaps we're frightened of our possibilities because we are frightened by the responsibilities of strength and success. Looking at ourselves honestly and objectively can be frightening. It often feels safer to simply follow the lead of others and do what is expected. So we mimic others and follow false roads. Our fear betrays both our talents and our responsibilities. We can only be ourselves, for better and for worse. Our weaknesses and our limits frighten and anger us, but they're simply part of us. Our strengths and talents are also part of us, and they may also frighten and anger us. You are responsible for yourself and your actions, for your strengths and your limits, and responsibility is hard.

Knowing yourself requires experience, reflection, and responsibility. Experience is required, because only experience can teach you what you love, what you find funny, what bores you, and what frightens you. You learn who you are by learning how you act and react. Simple experience, however, is not enough. While experience should enrich us and teach us to express ourselves more skillfully, life isn't so simple. Experience only teaches if we are willing to learn. Repeating the same mistakes doesn't enrich or deepen, and we all have our favored ways of failing to learn, such as denying consequences, blaming others, or diverting our attention with alcohol, television, or busyness. Experience that washes over you without being absorbed is wasted and lost. Wisdom comes from absorbing and pondering our experience.

But reflection alone is also not enough. You must translate your understanding into responsibilities. You cannot be anyone else, so be yourself wholeheartedly and responsibly. Take responsibility for your strengths and act strongly to do what you love. Take responsibility for your weaknesses and learn to protect yourself and others from them. Our weaknesses, not our strengths, do most of the damage. Many tasks will always challenge you, but you can learn to live with them and not to walk away from them. Maturing is never finished, but you are good enough, so relax. Knowing that you will be strong, gifted, and capable in some areas and weak, clumsy, and limited in other areas is simply having a good map of the territory of your life.

The costs of not knowing yourself

Knowing ourselves – having good maps – can be difficult. Our maps can be distorted by our fears and by our fantasies. Our maps may be sketchy and inaccurate because we are distracted and inattentive. We are often surprised by the sound of our voice on tape, the way we look on camera, or the comments we hear our friends make. It's not easy to be objective about ourselves. We want to give you a sense of the price you might pay for a poor map. We'll use our TDF language to create some examples, some object lessons, but the lessons extend beyond TDF.

Stereotyping yourself

We've met too many people who describe their TDF patterns as DDD, or TTT, or FFF. They mean to be funny, but they're in dangerous waters, because they are underestimating their abilities and talents. They are refusing responsibility. They are stereotyping and limiting themselves.

Marcia, for example, is a DFT executive. She knows she should value detailed analysis and planning. These are not her strengths, however, and are assuredly not the talents that brought her to her current position. No one ever promoted Marcia because she did brilliant, detailed planning. Simplifying, acting on limited information, and taking risks are the strengths that have brought her advancement. Planning and analysis feel clumsy and slow. She is tempted, then, to belittle planning and analysis and to work purely on gut feel and instinct. "That's not me," she'll say, "I'm not a planner. I'm a doer." In the short-run, this is easier, but disaster looms on the horizon. Planning and analysis will not create her success, but their absence will create her failure.

We are not asking Marcia to "become a TDF." That would be impossible. Marcia cannot see the world as a TDF sees the world. What we are asking her to do is to be a balanced and competent DFT. Marcia can plan and analyze. She won't do it in the same way a TDF would, because she sees the world differently, but she can learn to get the results she needs. This takes patience and discipline, but it's part of using all her talents. Marcia is stereotyping herself when she labels herself "not a planner." We all plan. Life gives us no other choice. Marcia simply needs to ask, "What kind of planning will work for me? What kind of planner can I be?"

Ignoring life's difficulties is irresponsible, but we are all tempted. DTFs and DFTs are tempted to *over-simplify* and to use action to avoid analysis or complexity. DTFs over-simplify by ignoring context, while DFTs over-simplify by ignoring data. When they see others reflecting and analyzing, trying to grasp consequences before plunging, or appreciating a situation without trying to do something, they may react defensively, by denying the complexity and with contempt for reflection and thoughtfulness. Shooting from the hip, acting without preparing sensibly, are signs of a DTF or DFT out of control.

TDFs and TFDs are tempted to *over-rationalize*, to ignore the unpredictable and spontaneous, to treat human issues impersonally, and to use plans to avoid the risks of the personal, the emotional, and the human. TDFs over-rationalize when they ignore the larger context of their factual world, while TFDs over-rationalize when they ignore the pressures of choices and refuse to act. The inevitable chaos and irrationality of complex interactions or intense actions defies their sense of the world, so they respond defensively, building more and more processes and more and more rules to try to organize, regiment, and control the chaos. Committees, study groups, memos, and policy papers are the result. Being right becomes more important than being effective. This is a TDF or TFD out of control.

FTDs and FDTs are tempted to *over-interpret*. FTDs over-interpret to avoid hard choices and FDTs over-interpret to avoid harsh realities and unpleasant facts. Their strengths so attune them to complexity and context, that they can find ambiguity anywhere. They can obsess about "what does it really mean?" rather than acting or withdrawing to a quiet place, alone, and focusing on narrow, important issues. Being sensitive and responsive becomes more important than being productive.

While simplifying, planning, and interpreting are strengths, they can become liabilities when they are used to evade the complexities and difficulties of the world. We cannot afford to limit ourselves to cartoon versions of our strengths and possibilities. When FDTs and DFTs act as if they live in a world without hard facts, they damage their capacity to deal with real constraints and rules, with planning and analysis. They end up feeling disorganized and out of control. When DTFs and TDFs act as if they live in a world free of connection and context, they damage their ability to deal with complexity, subtlety, and consequences. They end up feeling alienated and alone. And when FTDs and TFDs act as if they live in a world without choices and options, they damage their ability to deal with goals, deadlines, performance pressures, and authority. They end up feeling powerless and weak. We cannot allow ourselves to be cartoons and stereotypes.

Not seeing your strengths

We often have trouble seeing our talents and strengths. Perhaps it is too easy. We often undervalue our strengths, because they seem effortless. Anyone, we think, could do that, although this is not true. If Tanya makes cold calls comfortably, she may not see that others cannot. Or perhaps it is too risky. If we admit our strengths, we might have to act upon them and take responsibility for them. Or perhaps we delude ourselves by believing in an "ideal type," a single right way to behave, and we try to shape ourselves to that path. The world holds out many models of "ideal types." These models make seductive promises. If only you will be a cautious risk taker, who plans carefully and acts spontaneously, who disciplines firmly and is warmly loved, you will succeed. We are seduced. We try to mimic these models, we try to take their paths. This is tempting, but it can never work. We can only be ourselves. We can be ourselves successfully or we can be ourselves unsuccessfully. Those are our only choices.

An extreme example of trying to be someone else is what we call "masking." Sometimes, people try to live as if they were someone else. This sounds silly – "he's trying to pass as a TFD" – but the reality is sad. People who are really DFTs do try to live as TFDs, and people who are really FTDs do try to live as DTFs. They cannot change their perceptions, of course. A TDF can no more see the world in an FDT way than she can see oranges look purple or elephants look like daffodils. But we can *act* the roles and skills that belong more naturally to other patterns, while discarding the roles and skills that are naturally ours.

Masking isn't evil or immoral, but it is difficult, stressful, and finally pointless. When we're masking, we are always less than ourselves. DFTs just don't make very good TFDs. Masking is not the same as flexibility and adaptability. We need flexibility – a DFT sometimes needs to sit quietly and listen and a TFD sometimes needs to act on impulse – but masking is rigidity, not flexibility. Masking grows from fears, from trying to please others, and from not valuing yourself. The price, however, is high. Masking takes effort, and we feel this effort in our awkwardness, confusion, discomfort, or exhaustion. When we mask, we suffer a price.

Daniel is an FDT, for example, who came from a chaotic family that made security and stability very attractive. He chose to become an accountant, feeling that these skills would give him both security and stability. So far, so good. This may be a fine choice. But Daniel also felt that to be an accountant, he had to be a TDF. He didn't know our language, but he knew the reality. He saw people who looked calm, unharried, and deliberate. He saw them acting logically, step-by-step, and systematically, and he mistakenly saw being like this as the only road to security.

Daniel mastered accounting, but his effort to be a TDF made this a joyless and painful grind. He punished himself for his carelessness, his impetuosity, his restlessness. He planned compulsively and acted rigidly. What would be natural and comfortable for a TDF was a struggle for him. He didn't become a TDF; he became a stereotype. His rigidity and compulsivity have undermined his relationships and have created a ceiling for him at work. His problem is not accounting; his problem is the mask. His "solution" has become his problem.

We've worked with many people like Daniel who have tried to place themselves in alien patterns, often from early childhood. The start of real change for such people is recognizing their true patterns. They don't "change" patterns; they drop their masks. They don't feel they are becoming someone new; they feel they are coming home. They become themselves.

Daniel came to a TDF workshop believing he was a TDF. He tested as a TDF, because the *TDF Pattern Inventory* measures self-image, and he imaged himself as a TDF. His colleagues were less certain, however, sensing something not quite in line, and his behavior in the workshop was different than we expect of a TDF:

he expressed himself a bit too quickly; he engaged us a bit too readily; he spoke a bit too rapidly and smiled too easily. We didn't argue with him about his pattern. People have good reasons for behaving as they do and challenging Daniel without understanding his reasons would be irresponsible.

Over time, however, Daniel began to see that the FDT description fit him much better than the TDF description. He began to realize that his quickness to respond, his impetuosity, and his distaste for detail were not weaknesses but strengths. He stopped pretending to be a TDF accountant and began to explore the possibilities of being an FDT with excellent accounting skills. This was an enormous relief. The burden was lifted, and he began looking for ways to nurture and use his natural strengths. He found himself.

Most of us don't go to Daniel's lengths, but many of us think that we can succeed only by transforming our weaknesses into strengths. We see people do skillfully what feels impossible to us, so we suspect that if only we could do what they do, we would succeed. Vanessa for example, is a TFD executive who decided that the road to success lay in the aggressive improvising that she admired greatly in others. Because she is bright and talented, she can certainly *act* this part, but this is the wrong path for her. Her happiness and success will come through her strengths, not through her weaknesses. Vanessa is right to value improvising, but this will never be her best contribution. Her success must be built on her thoughtful and well-prepared consistency. Thoughtfulness and preparation, however, seem so easy to her that she fails to value her own strength.

Andrew, an FTD manager is awed by how his DTF colleague Sarah disciplines troublesome employees without obvious guilt and drives her people to perform. Andrew is intensely aware of his struggles with these responsibilities. He is not aware that Sarah envies how he wins the loyalty and affection of employees and customers. We watch others do with style and grace what we do painfully and clumsily. We think, "If only I could do that, then I would succeed." We don't notice the other person struggle with things that seem so easy for us. We forget that being imperfect is not a personal failure but the human condition.

One of the immediate benefits of a clearer image of ourselves, we've found, is what we call *growth by subtraction*. As we understand ourselves better, as we take responsibility for our strengths, we realize that we don't have to do everything. We can drop our fruitless efforts to be perfect and to be someone we can't be, and we can focus on being who we can be. This is a relief and a great step forward. We can give up the illusion of "If only..." and take responsibility for our real possibilities.

Taking responsibility for your strengths

Talent exacts a price; mediocrity is easier. Talent calls for responsibility. First, you are responsible for working hard to develop your talents by practicing and honing your skills. Then, you are responsible for the results of your efforts, for your work and your life. Sport is an interesting arena because it provides a visible platform for these responsibilities. We can see that immensely talented athletes succeed only because they work hard to develop their talents. We also see that the best athletes are those willing to take responsibility for the outcome of the game – to take the shot as the clock winds down, to risk the interception with a long pass, to hit when the game is on the line.

Knowing who you are is the first step in this ever-repeating cycle. The next step is taking responsibility. Knowing is a matter for the head, while responsibility is a matter for the heart. The words of the heart come harder, because accepting who you are requires paying a price. This is no longer a charming intellectual exercise. Now there are real stakes. Don't expect your friends, family, or employer to applaud when you act on your strengths. Talent has edges and creates friction. If you accept that you are a TFD, for example, you must take responsibility for your fascination with complex puzzles, for your cool aloofness, for your caution, and for your perfectionism. You can't just shrug these off as superficial habits which you may change one of these days. This is who you are and who you need to be. This is you.

Knowing your strengths, your possibilities, and your limits

Moving through life successfully requires realism. You must look in the mirror and be honest about what you see – honest about your strengths, about your possibilities, and about your limits. This honesty is the hardest part. Once you have begun to accomplish this, your strategy for succeeding is straightforward:

- Improve on your strengths;
- Explore your possibilities; and
- Protect yourself and others from your weaknesses

Building on your strengths

Your responsibilities to yourself and to those who depend upon you begin with your strengths, because your strengths carry you. Recognizing your own strengths, as we have seen, can be difficult. We may focus so intently on our failings that we don't notice our successes, or we may confuse our wishes with our accomplishments. Ask yourself some difficult questions:

- What have I done well?
- What have others told me I have done well?
- What have I done that I enjoyed?
- What have I done that has shown concrete, tangible results?

This sounds like a job interview, doesn't it? In a sense, it is. You are looking for the jobs, the relationships, and the responsibilities where you can succeed. Any good job interviewer knows that candidates will try to respond with vague generalities – like, "I'm good with people" – and any good interviewer will press for specifics, for details, and for examples. What are the strengths you have recognized in yourself on the job, at home, or in your community? Perhaps you're using your best strengths with your Little League team. Great. Now how can you use them elsewhere as well?

We hope that we have been expanding your sense of what counts as strengths. Most jobs, for example, can be done well in a variety of ways, using different strengths. Consider three different project managers for a software development firm, all of whom are successful, but all of whom succeed from different strengths. Jason is a TFD who has found that he succeeds by his calm, his diplomacy, and his tracking of details. Andrea is an FDT who has based her success on recruiting and enlisting talent, juggling pieces, and motivating and persuading with drama. Mario is a DTF who succeeds by being demanding, sifting out the irrelevant requests and requirements, and focusing on clear milestones. Each has found a path to success, and each has found that mimicking someone else would be a disaster. We are not saying these managers are interchangeable parts. Their strengths best fit different kinds of projects. TFD Jason is best with long-term projects that require managing demanding publics. FDT Andrea is best with projects that require high talent "prima donnas." DTF Mario is best with projects with high performance pressures and tight deadlines.

As another example, consider three sales people. Carmen is a TDF who creates and follows clear plans, studies her customers, and studies her products. Walter is an FTD who pleases customers, interprets their needs, and builds customer loyalty. Linda is a DFT who sells hope and possibilities with passion. They all succeed, although each succeeds best with a different kind of sales. TDF Carmen sells technical products where her expertise gives her crucial credibility. FTD Walter sells in a retail setting where repeat sales are key. DFT Linda sells high-ticket, high-emotion, high-impact advertising services. Most sales training seems intent on making everyone sell in the same way, so many people think they can't sell because sales "experts" have convinced them that imitating FDTs is the only road to success, just as project management models have held up TDFs as the model to follow. Yet people differ, customers differ, and products differ. Different roads can lead to success.

Ignore all advice to be like someone else. Don't worry about who you "ought" to be; discover who you are. Find what you do well and do it better. That is the best advice we know.

Exploring your possibilities

While we need to be ourselves, we often have too narrow an image of ourselves. Don't confuse realism with pessimism or cynicism. Realism encourages and supports exploring your possibilities; pessimism and cynicism encourage stagnation and immobility. We've talked already about how we stereotype ourselves. Breaking from our self-imposed limits is exciting, because we can be more than we are. You have limits, but you also have more talents than you will ever have the time to fully develop.

We want to offer you a simple and widely used map of your possibilities to check whether you are developing your full range of possibilities and to identify new areas to explore. Skills are often divided into three groups – information skills, task skills, and people skills. You have abilities in all three of these skill clusters, but you may not see this. You may see yourself too narrowly. We've found that many people think we are claiming that TFDs and TDFs specialize in information skills, that DFTs and DTFs specialize in task skills, and that FTDs and FDTs specialize in people skills. This is a terrible form of stereotyping. All six patterns have the potential to develop information, task, and people skills. This is a good way to measure yourself, to see if your skills span all these possibilities.

All six patterns can handle information with great skill, but these skills differ across the patterns.

- TDFs are analytic; they break information into chunks; they create outlines and classifications; they clarify and define; they arrange information in sequence; they order information.

- TFDs are data-driven; they learn by absorbing and slowly assimilating; they value completeness and thoroughness; they index information; they track information; they specialize and become expert.

- FTDs form impressions by absorbing large amounts of information and giving it context and unity; they give perspective and a sense of values to information; they prefer the concrete and the tangible; they learn by discussion and interaction.

- FDTs learn from stories, anecdotes, and metaphors; they create images to unify information into a dramatic symbol; they see information as personal, subjective, and contextual; they engage and interact with information.

- DFTs skim information, seeking ideas and concepts; they think divergently, generating multiple responses to a single input; they are action learners using trial-and-error; they are comfortable with fragmentary and incomplete data.

- DTFs are critical learners, learning by argument and disagreements; they sift information quickly, looking for a core truth they can carry away; they focus on content, not context; they have to know the conclusion before they can evaluate the evidence.

These skills differ dramatically, but they are all legitimate ways to handle information. If you believe that the TDF way, for example, is the "correct" way to handle information, you are indirectly labeling the other five patterns as stupid or incompetent. This is not simply unfair; it is also untrue. Anyone who has achieved a high level of competency in one of these sets knows how to handle information. One key question to ask yourself here is, "How do I learn?" Many of us don't learn by following the models our schools held up for us. Neither FDTs nor DFTs gain much from sitting through a lecture, for example, and TDFs don't find discussions terribly helpful. There is no one right way to learn, just as there is no one right way to sell or manage a project. Your task is to find the ways that work best for you and to find the settings in which you learn best. You're an adult now. You don't have to follow someone else's rules.

Similarly, in approaching tasks and actions, the six patterns have different possible strengths:

- TDFs are planners, organizers, preparers, and delegators.
- TFDs are precise, consistent, cautious, tactical, and well rehearsed.
- FTDs are coordinators, stabilizers, harmonizers, fitters, and process-centered.
- FDTs are jugglers, implementers, enrollers, and energetic.
- DFTs are strategizers, improvisors, focusing on novelty and possibility.
- DTFs are authorities, focused on goals, relentless, and driving.

And once again, anyone who has mastered one of these skill sets has valuable tools for operating in the world of tasks and actions. Complex tasks can often be performed in more than one way, although, as we've said before, not every task can be done with equal success by every style. This is worth thought and experimentation. Can you do the task in front of you in your way? If not, perhaps you are the wrong person to do that task. Find tasks that fit your strengths.

Finally, all six patterns can work well with people.

- TDFs succeed with others because they are seen as fair, credible, steady, reliable, and very skilled at structured, planned interactions.

- TFDs succeed with others because they are seen as diplomatic, thoughtful, calm, accepting, and nonjudgmental.

- FTDs succeed with others because they are seen as sensitive, receptive, trustworthy, nurturing, and caring, as great listeners and sources of support.

- FDTs succeed with others because they're seen as engaging, personal, interactive, fun, and charming, as great talkers and energizers.

- DFTs succeed with people because they're seen as stimulating, engaged, intense, unpredictable, and persuasive.

- DTFs succeed with people because they're seen as responsible, strong, direct, forceful, candid, and frank.

We're asking you, once again, to expand your sense of "people skills." We often stereotype people skills as the "warm and fuzzy stuff." Interacting, working, and living with others go far beyond this stereotype.

Protecting your vulnerabilities

While we encourage exploring your possibilities, we also know that you have limitations and weaknesses. We know this because you are human and perfection is not available to humans. Your strengths and your weaknesses grow from the same soil, so you cannot eliminate your weaknesses without undermining your strengths. You cannot both improvise brilliantly and plan brilliantly, because the talents that support one block the other. To improvise truly well, you must see the world differently than you must see it to plan well. Similarly, you cannot both focus intensely and see the big-picture. Again, the talents that support one block the other. Your weaknesses come in the same package as your strengths.

Your weaknesses are inevitable, but they pose problems. Your weaknesses can hurt you. We've rejected the fallacy that "fixing" your weaknesses will help you succeed, but ignoring your weaknesses will cause you to fail. DFTs fail when they take thoughtless risks; DTFs fail when they are blindsided by events outside their focus; TDFs fail when they ignore the social setting in which they work; TFDs fail when they wait too long for the last piece of information; FTDs fail when they try to please everyone; and FDTs fail when they don't plan or organize.

An FDT will not succeed by buying a larger calendar and a TDF will not succeed by networking more, but an FDT has to find ways to protect himself against his spontaneity and a TDF has to find ways to protect herself against her tight task-focus. You will have weaknesses, but you do not have to be irresponsible about them. We want to make some suggestions here about how to be responsible about your weaknesses.

First, don't take yourself so seriously. You are not always perfect. Sometimes your actions are foolish and silly and any sane person would laugh at you. So laugh. A little humor is a powerful tool. If you can be amused by your failings, you are less likely to damage yourself and others. You are less likely to be defensive, rigid, secretive, and angry. You are less likely to punish others for your shortcomings. You are less likely to attack others for doing what you cannot do. You are less likely to insist that you can do what you cannot do. This is our best advice.

Second, be kind to yourself. You will have to operate from your weaknesses on many occasions, so you will feel clumsy and inadequate and uncertain, but give yourself the opportunity to perform as well as you can. Recognize that you need more time and more space to work from weakness than to work from strength. If you are a TFD, and you are being pushed to make rapid choices from incomplete information, you are working from weakness. Don't try to respond too quickly. Say, "I need three minutes," walk away and stare at a blank wall and consider your options. Then return and choose. Three minutes is very little time, but it will help immensely.

Third, experiment. Try new behaviors to increase your flexibility, but only try these new behaviors in low-stake situations, where you can tolerate failing. Here are some of our favorite experiments.

- TDFs – go to lunch with a co-worker and don't discuss work, sports, or hobbies.
- TFDs – deliberately make small errors, like wearing mismatching socks.
- FTDs – ask out loud during a conversation, "So what's in it for me?"
- FDTs – go to a large gathering and be a wallflower; just observe.
- DFTs – sit still and reflect on a recent experience; what did you learn?
- DTFs – ask for help in doing some task.

Try these experiments simply to make your weaknesses less frightening. There may be other lessons to be learned. Try and see.

Finally, remember that you are not in this alone. Where you are weak, others are strong, and you can borrow their strengths. DTF Georgia has trouble reading the political currents in her organization, but she regularly lunches with her FTD friend Chandra to get her perspective. TFD Luis uses his DFT friend Milton to push him into action. FDT Nick likes to run his plans past his TDF friend Debbie to see if he is being clear and thorough. We get by with a little help from our friends. Depending is not dependency, because we can help each other. Adults can depend on each other and help each other. This is the glory of human community. This is why we live and work in groups and organizations.

Being your best

People have been striving to make the most of their lives and their talents for many thousands of years. Wise men and women have reflected long on this task; great men and women have succeeded in this task. There are no mysteries or secret formulas. The task is simple to understand but difficult to live. We have spelled out the rules for you; that is the easy part. You have to act upon them; that is the difficult part. First, and most difficult, you have to know yourself. You have to look in the mirror and be honest. You have to know your talents and your limits; you have to know your possibilities and your impossibilities. Then build on your strengths, explore your possibilities, and protect yourself from your vulnerabilities.

There is a rhythm to this process, a rhythm of alternating reflection and action. You stop to ponder your image in the mirror, then you act to build, explore, and protect, and then you come back to ponder again. If you neglect either pole of this rhythm – if you reflect without acting or if you act without reflecting – your efforts will come to nothing. So ask yourself one more question. Where are you vulnerable? Will you fail to reflect or will you fail to act? This too is part of the map.

13

Reading other people

The best tool for living and working with others is to try to see from their perspectives: trying to read how they see the world and trying to see how they read us.

Jack was a new manager in his corporation's tax department, and unwittingly he was creating confusion and chaos. He liked to wander around the department, dropping into people's cubicles and chatting with them about nothing in particular, just to get to know them and to stay in touch. He was a good FTD manager, doing what good FTD managers do. He was getting to know his people, building connections, and tending his garden. In this particular organization, however, FTD managers were rare and Jack's style was new to his people. They panicked. They couldn't figure out what he was doing. Was he spying? Was he taunting? Was he softening them up for bad news? When we taught the department about TDF, there was a moment in the workshop when people realized that Jack was an FTD, and everyone just went "Ohhhhhh." The relief in the room was palpable. They had begun to understand. And Jack had begun to understand as well.

Jack was practicing what we preach: he understood his strengths as an FTD and he was working from those strengths. He wasn't mimicking a style that didn't fit him; he was being himself. But Jack's actions had results that he didn't desire or even understand. He certainly didn't intend to stir up turmoil. As an FTD, Jack valued harmony, and he couldn't understand why his actions were creating disruption and fear.

We don't live, work, or succeed alone. Our actions touch others and their actions touch us. We bump, we jostle, we embrace, we help, we frustrate, we annoy, and we delight each other. And often we are – like Jack – completely mystified about the effects of our actions. Knowing yourself and making the right choices requires knowing something about other people, because people are the most important part of the territory through which you are moving. You need to know something about how you affect them and how they affect you. Your actions, reactions, and interactions with others are crucial to your journey. For all his skills, Jack was blind to how he affected his employees, blind to how others saw him. To be himself successfully, Jack needs to read his human setting more skillfully, if only so he will know how to protect himself better.

Your first step is to see that people truly are different. We once knew someone who thought that if you suddenly awoke an Englishman in the middle of the night he would speak "regular" English. We are all like this friend of ours; we are all "pattern chauvinists." We expect others to speak and act as we would speak and act. We don't really believe that other people see the world differently. We believe that our perceptions are the real and true perceptions and that other people are simply mistaken or misinformed. We believe that if other people would listen to us carefully, they would recognize the superiority of our perceptions. We don't really want to believe that people are different – that our way is not the only way – and we trip over our false assumptions. Jack assumed that his employees saw his efforts as he saw them, but just as you need to give up unrealistic expectations and fantasies of yourself, you also need to give up unrealistic expectations and fantasies of others.

People in Jack's position often ask us, "I'm an FTD and I have to deal with a TDF, so how do I do that?" Often they really mean, "How can I get this person to be more like me, to act the way I want her to act?" We are happy to say that this is an impossible request. People are different and that is not going to change and should not change. Other people are going to be themselves and not extensions of our wishes and desires. They will confuse, puzzle, and challenge you. You cannot change this, nor should you wish to change this. If you begin to see how you and others affect each other, however, you can change *your* actions to create better interactions.

Our goal in this chapter is not to offer advice on love and friendship or power and influence. Our intent is more modest. We want to help you read other people more successfully. If Jack came to us, we would suggest that he ask himself a single question: *"What does this situation look like to the other person?"* Asking this question is not a simple formula for "winning friends and influencing people." There are no simple formulas. Since people are not machines, we cannot tell you what buttons to push to get the responses you want. Trying to answer this question, however, should help you make wiser choices in your interactions with others.

This question is simple to ask but difficult to answer, so we want to spend this chapter looking at this question. Answering the question, however tentatively, requires an act of imagination. You must try to see the world from the other person's perspective. You must try to stand in their place. You won't always succeed, but the effort is always worthwhile. Psychologists call this act of imagination "role taking," and they've found that it drives the social and moral development of children. This act of imagining also defines maturity in adults. As we develop these skills, we come to see ourselves from the outside, to see ourselves through others' eyes, and to understand how we affect others. This is a great gift.

Guessing people's patterns

Knowing someone else's TDF pattern can help you. Knowing someone's pattern can give you a better map of your interactions. In settings where TDF has become a common language, people assure us that this is true. People even post their patterns on their desks to help others interact with them more successfully. This can be fun, but most of the time, you won't have this kind of help, so people often ask us for a list of clues so that they can recognize other people's TDF patterns and respond to them in the best possible ways. This is logical, but we don't know how to do it. Recognizing patterns is a tricky business. We like to say that there are only three people who can do it, but each of us has doubts about the other two. Recognizing patterns is just a small part of the more basic skill of reading people well.

We'll give you some hints on making pattern guesses, but first we want to focus on the difficulties, because they point out some difficulties in reading people and acting responsibly requires accepting these difficulties. People are not simple. There are good reasons why we have trouble reading people. When we first started trying to assess and measure patterns, many years ago, we tried several methods. We tried both *self-report* – having you describe yourself – and *other-report* – having other people describe you. What we found was that self-report worked well and that other-report worked poorly. Self-report formats have many well-known problems in measuring psychological characteristics: we're all good at fooling both ourselves and others, and it's easy to answer questions to look as you wish you were or as you think others want you to be. These are serious problems and much of the technical literature on psychological measurement has focused on them. In our work, however, we found greater problems with *other-reports*. Other people will not only disagree with you about what your pattern is, but they also won't agree with each other. If we ask three different people to describe you, we will often end up with descriptions that fit three different patterns. This inconsistency led us to drop our efforts in this direction.

We see similar things every day. In organizations where TDF is widely used and known, people will come to a workshop saying that their friends have told them about TDF and have also told them that their pattern is FTD or whatever. They arrive curious to see if their friends were right about them. And often, to their great delight, they find that their friends were wrong. Why are they delighted? Because we don't want to believe that we're simple and transparent. We like to think that we're mysterious and misunderstood. Why were their friends wrong? That's more interesting.

We make mistakes in reading people for a number of reasons. First, TDF patterns describe perceptions and only indirectly describe actions. Second, we routinely confuse people's roles and their personalities. We stereotype people. Finally, we assume that our interaction with another person fully represents him, and that may not work.

Let's start with the first issue. We can't see other people's perceptions; we can only see their actions. As we've already seen, actions grow out of perceptions, but this is indirect and complex. People's actions don't precisely mirror their perceptions. This is why you can assess your own pattern more successfully than others can. You know what your world looks like, but I can only guess what yours is like, based on how I've seen you act.

We also routinely confuse roles and personality. We're all prone to assuming that our accountants are TFDs, our mothers are FTDs, and our bosses DTFs. Maybe so, but maybe not. We're much too quick to stereotype. We even stereotype ourselves. People walk into TDF workshops assuming that because they are computer programmers they must be TFDs, or because they are salespeople they must be FDTs, or because they are executives they must be DTFs. If we do this to ourselves, imagine what we do to others. People are not their roles. When people are behaving consistently with their roles – when a copier repair specialist pokes inside a copier or a real estate salesperson "chats up" a prospect – this tells you very little about them. It only tells you about their role. You learn more when people act inconsistently with their roles – when the repair specialist chats rather than pokes or the salesperson spends more time with a spreadsheet than with prospects. Inconsistencies of this sort are wonderful clues about people. When people behave as we expect, we may be seeing the role and not the person. When they surprise us, when they act "out of role," they are showing us much more about themselves than they do when they fit our stereotypes.

Our third shortcoming in reading people is that we assume that our interaction with the other person fully describes him. We assume that if we only see Carl in church that he must be very religious and if we only see Tony in bars that he must be a drunk. Remember that Carl also only sees us in church and Tony only sees us in bars. Our interactions with people are usually a thin slice of their lives. That can be misleading. You are not describing Carl and Tony; you are describing your perspectives on them. People are complicated. If you think they are simple, it is only because your interactions with them are simple. If you saw them in a greater variety of settings, your perspectives might be more complex.

So how do you make guesses about people's patterns? The best rule is to pay less attention to *what* they are doing and more attention to *how* they are doing it. When a salesperson approaches you at a car dealer, you don't know what pattern she is. There are successful car sales people of every pattern. But as she begins to sell, she will begin to show you more about herself. *How* she sells begins to tell you about her: does she begin by focusing on the car you're looking at or upon you? Does she engage quickly or slowly? Does she talk or does she listen? Does she speak quickly or slowly? We show ourselves in *how* we act.

Another important clue is to look for behaviors that surprise you or seem not to fit the situation or the roles the person is playing. We mentioned this earlier. Inconsistencies and surprises are great clues. We focus on consistencies, but this is a mistake. When you are surprised or puzzled, take your reactions seriously. Your puzzlement means that your assumptions aren't working. We notice our differences precisely because we surprise each other. Our interactions don't go as we expect. People act in ways that surprise us and we seem to confuse them. We bump. One of the best places to begin sorting out pattern differences and pattern effects is in our surprises and bumps.

Most importantly, look for clues about how the other person sees the world. We display our perceptions in our actions and in our words, in what we do and don't do, in what we say and don't say. Learning to read how people are displaying their perceptions requires attention and imagination, and one of the values of a tool like TDF is that it encourages you to look more closely and listen more closely. In the end, the looking and the listening are the true secrets. Even if you can't guess their patterns, you will know more about them.

"What does this situation look like to the other person?"

We display our perceptions in our words, in our actions, and in our choices. You read my actions and choices, and I read yours. How we read each other is worth a great deal of thought. The way I read you may be very different than you imagine, and the way you read me may be very different than I imagine, because how we read each other is also shaped by our perceptions. A DFT displays his perceptions differently than does a TFD and an FTD reads you differently than a TDF does. We focus on different aspects of the world.

Let's create a simple metaphor to understand how we interact and read each other. We'll define three kinds of information – which we'll call T-information, D-information, and F-information – to clarify our interactions. This is simplistic, but we've found it helpful.

T information is factual and objective. The pronoun here is *It*. When we work from our T lens, we focus on the world of things, objects, topics, tasks, and issues. This world is objective and impersonal, centered on the objects that are "out there," independent of us. In this sphere, the personal, the subjective, the impressionistic, and the non-factual are simply noise and serve to obscure and distort the true message. A spreadsheet is a beautiful display of T information. T information focuses on the words we use. Our shorthand term for this class of information will be *content*.

D information is choices and options. The pronoun here is *I*. Working from the D lens, I see a world that consists of *my* choices, *my* interests, and *my* responsibilities. I also see that you have a world consisting of *your* choices, *your* interests, and *your* responsibilities. This information is simple and black-and-white. Anything that obscures the simplicity and the clarity of these choices is noise; anything that introduces gray to this black-and-white world is distorting. "Yes or No" is the basic message. D information is displayed in our choices and our actions. We'll call this kind of information *conclusions*.

F-information is connections and linkages. The pronoun here is *We*. In this realm, we see the relationships among people and events as the center of interest. We focus on the connections among events, the connections among people, and the settings in which the events and the people interact and connect. This information elaborates; this information finds the meaning of any event in its connections to other events. Anything that severs or limits those connections is a distortion of the message. A story or an anecdote displays this information beautifully. F information focuses on the settings and styles we choose. We'll call this information *context*.

We share the information that seems most important to us and we ignore the information that seems least important; this shapes our displays. This also shapes how we read others' displays. If Winston is an FDT, for example, his first impulse will be to display the important contextual information he sees by telling stories and drawing verbal pictures to capture the connections he sees. He will try to connect to the person he is talking with. He will not focus on the accuracy of his facts or the choices he sees, because these seem less compelling. If Stephanie, on the other hand, is a TDF, she may see Winston's stories as pointless, his efforts to connect to her as invasive, and his neglect of facts as distressing. She is looking for content, which Winston is not providing, and she is ignoring context, which he is providing in abundance. Winston is going to feel misread and misunderstood, while Stephanie is going to feel frustrated and irritated. They focus on different information and this raises barriers between them.

How we display our perceptions

Let's look at some simple examples of how we display our perceptions. Imagine a problem at work. Your customer-service workstations have developed a glitch that cuts customers off in the middle of their phone calls on a random but annoyingly frequent basis. You are not a technician, but you are your company's liaison to the telecommunications and hardware contractors. Your boss wishes to encourage you to take action on this situation. How will she do this?

Stop and use your imagination. If your boss is a TDF, how will she give you this order? If she is a DFT, how will she do this? If she is an FTD? What will these different displays look like? Won't a TDF create a display that stresses content more than context? Won't a DFT create a display that stresses conclusions more than content? And won't an FTD create a display that stresses context more than conclusions?

Here's one TDF scenario: "There seems to be some sort of problem with the CS workstations. Get a clear description of the problem from the supervisors and then get with the venders and figure out what this problem is. See if you can get some sort of short-term fix so we can keep the stations up, then get back to me with some ideas about a long-term solution so this won't recur."

Here's one DFT scenario: "Hey, the CS workstations are cutting people off. Get this fixed."

And here's one FTD scenario: "Have you got a minute? Have you heard that there's some sort of problem with the CS workstations? Well, you're the guy who knows all the players, so why don't you talk to some people and see who you need to get together with, so that we can help these folks. Does this make sense to you?"

Remember that we said to pay attention to *how* people do things. These three bosses are approaching the same problem with the same agenda, but their styles are quite distinct. These differences, however, are not casual or superficial, so let's analyze these scenarios and ponder their lessons. Each boss is *displaying* her perception of the situation. Different patterns send different unspoken messages in these situations, different *subtexts*, and these unspoken messages carry great weight in the total message, conveying each boss's different perceptions and assumptions. Each boss gives her order to show what she wants:

In the TDF scenario, the boss wants the problem defined and solutions distinguished. She wants action, but first she wants information. She is not giving detailed instructions, but she is defining what are the acceptable responses to the situation. She wants clarity and competency. She wants you to see *how* she wants the job done.

The DFT boss is both vaguer and more abrupt. She specifies a goal – what she wants done – and lets it go at that. She says nothing about how to do it, because she doesn't care how it gets done, just so it gets done. She communicates urgency – this is important, so get it done now – and she wants action. She wants you to see *what* she wants done.

The FTD boss wants participation and interaction to build commitment and concern. She asks questions and invites response. She discusses roles and responsibilities, not instructions and not outcomes. Who should be doing what and why they should be doing it are her concerns. She wants consensus and commitment. She wants you to see *why* she wants your help.

How others read us

Each of our bosses is saying what she wants, but this does not mean that her employees are hearing what she wants. *The most fundamental rule in communicating is that it is not what is said that matters, but what is heard.* In our examples, each boss is giving an order that reflects how she sees the situation. The TDF believes that action follows clarity; the DFT believes that action is driven by urgency; and the FTD believes that action grows from commitment. And each is correct. Clarity, urgency, and commitment are all important. If you read each boss well, you will see how the situation has engaged her, and you will be able to do as she is asking. We don't, however, always read each other well. If you misread her, your response will irritate her, no matter how good your intentions.

When we listen, we try to read the other person's perceptions. We fail to read people well for many reasons – such as lack of interest and attention, anxiety, stereotypes and preconceptions, distractions and noise – but some of our failures are rooted in our perceptual patterns. We have strong biases about *how* we attend, because we have strong biases about what people must be trying to say. We assume that they are trying to communicate what we would be trying to communicate. We focus too narrowly on the kinds of information we value. Our TDF friend Stephanie focuses on content, and when she hears little content from Winston, she assumes he is saying nothing.

Consider how different employees might hear the TDF order that we have sketched, asking for a definition of the problem and a proposal for solutions. A DFT may listen impatiently and restlessly. *Just tell me what you want and let's get on with it.* He does not hear the urgency he wants. He hears, "I don't trust you to do this the right way." He is looking for a conclusion. An FTD on the other hand may feel shut out. *Hang on, can't we just talk about this a moment, bounce a few ideas off each other?* He does not hear the connection he wants. He hears "I don't value you enough to discuss this with you." He is looking for context. Both the DFT and FTD may feel insulted or patronized by the insistence on instructions and procedures. *Do you think I'm too stupid to figure this out?* They hear pointless clarity.

Or consider the DFT order to just fix it. A TDF may feel that the order is altogether too vague. *What do you mean "fix it"? Fix it how? Long-term, short-term, on-the-cheap, whatever-it-takes, what?* He doesn't hear the content and clarity he wants. An FTD is likely to hear this order as simply rude. *And you're not even going to ask if I can do this?* He doesn't hear the context and connection he wants. Both the TDF and the FTD may feel imposed upon by this urgency. *Okay, this is important. So were the last seven things you told me to do. Which should I do first?* They hear pointless urgency. Both will go away, only to return shortly to seek clarification and input, thereby irritating the DFT who can't believe these people can't follow simple orders without all this hand holding.

Finally, consider the FTD order asking for cooperation and commitment. A DFT may not even hear an order – *Okay, maybe I'll get to it next week* – because he doesn't hear conclusions and urgency. Questions don't sound like orders. A TDF may feel irritated by the lack of structure and clarity. *What? I'm supposed to guess what to do? I'm supposed to do your job?* Both the DFT and the TDF hear a lack of direction in the FTD's orders. *Yeah, okay, I know these people. So what? Why are we talking about this?* They hear pointless context.

What others hear may not be what we thought we were saying. What we see clearly, others may not see at all. What we see as central, others may not value. *How* we speak and interact may be sending important messages that we don't even notice. No wonder we spend so much of our lives feeling that no one is listening.

Helping others feel heard

Our daily interactions often feel confusing and challenging because we read one another poorly. I assume that you see what I see, and I expect you to want what I want. I become confused when you don't act as I think you should, and you become confused because I don't act as you think I should. We assume, and then we act on our bad assumptions about each other.

Let's look at an example. Consider Tim, a DFT marketing specialist who works with Sam, a TFD. Tim goes home at night raging because Sam is still analyzing and still collecting data for a direct-mail campaign that Tim knows will work. Tim feels it's time to stop analyzing and to start selling. Sam, on his side, goes home with headaches and a knotted stomach because he fears Tim's irresponsibility. There is simply too much uncertainty to justify moving on this campaign yet, and he feels that the entire weight of acting like a responsible grown-up has been thrust onto him. This conflict is like stepping on the brake and the gas at the same time. DFT Tim is ready to go, but TFD Sam wants to study the issue more carefully.

In listening to Sam, DFT Tim is listening for conclusions. Content, for Tim, only makes sense when it supports conclusions. Sam, however, is not offering any conclusions. This is difficult for Tim to hear, so he assumes that Sam is concluding that the risk is too high and the campaign should be dumped. Tim is misreading Sam. But Sam is also misreading Tim. He thinks that Tim is rejecting his content, so Sam responds by piling on more content. Tim, however, is not rejecting Sam's content; he's rejecting what he assumes is Sam's conclusion. Tim listens impa-

tiently, trying to speed Sam to a conclusion. Sam listens very patiently – although with frustration – hoping that Tim will give
him some content. Tim thinks they are talking about conclusions, while Sam thinks they are talking about content. They are
not hearing each other.

You cannot be successful with people over time without
making them feel heard and making them feel valued. This isn't
always enough, of course, but it is always a start. Everyone wants
to be heard; everyone wants to be understood; everyone wants to
be given attention. This is a fundamental truth about all of us.
When we are misunderstood, when someone reads us poorly, we
are deeply offended. The issue becomes the apparent lack of attention and respect. Notice in our examples how often people
feel insulted.

The human truth is that all of us want to be understood and
heard and valued. We're less interested in understanding and
hearing and valuing. Tim is working hard to make Sam understand him, just as Sam is working hard to make Tim understand.
Neither is working hard enough to understand the other. When
we talk about improving our "communication skills" or our "relationship skills," we usually mean getting other people to understand *us* better. There is, however, an important phrase that
describes people who reverse these priorities and try first to understand the other person. That phrase is *grown up*. Being a
grown up, in this context, suggests taking responsibility for
making the interaction work.

Reading others more skillfully

Your first responsibility is to read the other person as well as
you can. Tim and Sam need to read each other better. This is not
idealism. Tim cannot make realistic choices about how to work
with Sam as long as he is misreading Sam. Tim's anger is not
realistic: it is not a response to reality; it is a response to his assumptions. If you assume that the other person is seeing things
as you see them, you will make bad choices. Your key tool is

reading the other person, trying to understand what he wants and what the issues look like to him. Reading comes first.

The key skill in reading people is *active listening*. The phrase "active listening" is intended to avoid the illusion that we are listening just because sounds are entering our ears. Listening is not the passive act of hearing. Listening is an active effort to understand. Every book on communication sings the praises of active listening, because this is the single most important and powerful interpersonal skill. That's a strong statement, but the evidence is clear.[*]

The heart of active listening is paying attention to what the other person is saying. If you're thinking about what you're going to say next or where you're going to have dinner, you're not listening. If you're fidgeting or playing with your desk toys or reading your e-mail, you're not listening. Most importantly, if you're talking, you're not listening. If the other person believes that you are not paying attention, you've lost and insulted her. On the other hand, if she believes that you are paying attention, you've built significant credibility. Few actions are more powerful than attention. Think of how often you've heard powerful and successful people praised for focusing on the other person as if he were the only person in the world. Attention is powerful.

The greatest enemy of good listening is the pressure we feel to respond. Tim is thinking about how to push Sam forward and Sam is thinking about how to slow Tim down. Tim is listening to Tim and Sam is listening to Sam. They aren't listening to each other. This is not a dialogue; this is two monologues. Tim should focus less on persuading Sam and more on understanding Sam.

---

[*] We're only going to sketch how to listen actively. We want to sharpen your interest in this skill, but you cannot learn this skill – or any skill – from a book. You need opportunities to practice and to receive feedback and suggestions. You need coaching. There are many resources for this coaching, such as corporate training programs and community colleges, that we encourage you to explore.

He should shut up and listen. Then if he decides that Sam is saying nothing of importance, he will have realistic grounds for making some choices about working with Sam.

When you're trying to understand someone, trying to read them, you want as much information from him as you can absorb. Listening is your tool. You should only speak for three reasons. First, you should make occasional sounds and gestures to show that you are listening and to *encourage* the other person to continue. Then, you should periodically *summarize* what the other person has said in your own words, without elaborating, editorializing, judging, or correcting. This shows that you have heard what he is saying and checks that you have heard accurately. Finally, you should ask questions to *clarify* points you don't understand. Your goal is not to challenge or counter but to clarify and understand. And that's it. Encourage, summarize, and clarify. If you do nothing else, you will improve your interactions with others dramatically.

Let's look at these skills more closely. Matthew, for example, is a TDF manager who is weak at encouraging others, at making it easier and more rewarding for them to speak with him. Matthew is an observer who values some distance when interacting, but his disengaged style is often read as a lack of interest, even when he is most interested. He realized that he wasn't getting information he needed to succeed because his people didn't feel comfortable talking with him. He said that his door was always open, but few of his employees came through that door. With some coaching from a friend, Matthew learned that leaning forward, making eye contact, and nodding his head was more encouraging and receptive than leaning back and staring at the ceiling. He still feels a bit silly and artificial when he consciously encourages people, but it's paying off.

Similarly, Rosemary has learned the values of summarizing. Rosemary is an FTD supervisor whose people do regularly talk with her. She began to feel uncomfortable, however, with these talks. They just didn't feel business-like enough. She enjoyed the talks, but she has a department to run and the talks felt too casual and unfocused. She found that summarizing every few minutes helped her stay focused and helped her feel more useful to her people.

Finally, Amy is a DFT manager who realized that she was walking away from discussions without having pulled enough content from them. As a small-T, she does not focus on content during interactions, and she realized this was hurting her. To focus herself, she began to ask clarifying questions about content. She would ask, "What specific information suggests this?" or "Could you give me an example of what you mean?" She's found that this helps her in reading content. Similarly, if she needed more information about conclusions, she might ask, "Could you summarize for me what's most important here?" or "What do you see as our choices here?" Or to get greater clarity about context, she might ask, "What's the story here? How did this happen?" or "How's this going to effect how we work here?" Once you recognize that you neglect one kind of information, you can work to get strong in that arena.

Remember that we said the key question you should ask yourself is, "What does this situation look like to the other person?" Listening should answer this question. Neither Tim nor Sam has listened well. They are stuck inside their own perceptions and assumptions. If they were reading each other better, they would realize that they had common ground as well as disagreements. They both want the campaign to succeed, for example, and they both want some credit for this success. They both want to be recognized as valuable contributors. They both want to be heard. There are real differences between them as well, but they might be more manageable if they first recognized the common ground.

Or perhaps it won't work. Perhaps the other person is too entrenched or too rigid or too frightened to explore the possibili-

ties. At least you will understand that. Often this advice seems
too easy: it's not dramatic enough and it doesn't cast us in the
starring role. All of this is true. Listening is not glamorous; it is
only realistic.

Helping others read your message

Your first responsibility is to read others as well as you can.
Your second responsibility is to help others read you. This means
realizing that *how* you communicate may be an obstacle to others. What is obvious to you may not be obvious to others. If you
are a TDF, for example, there are predictable ways that your
style can hurt you as well as help you in communicating with
others. Remember, once more, that your communication is measured not by what you say but by what others hear.

This would be simplest, as we said early in this chapter, if
you knew the perceptual pattern of the person you were working
with. For example, if you are speaking with a TDF, you would be
heard best if you framed your message in facts, delivering a concrete, logical, and evidence-filled presentation. You want to provide clear structure, minimize emotional appeal, and maximize
content. TDFs are persuaded by evidence, which means facts and
solid methods. They value precision in the use of facts, numbers,
and language, and you will lose credibility if you are sloppy with
any of these. When Sgt. Joe Friday asked for "Just the facts,
ma'am" on *Dragnet*, he spoke for TDFs everywhere. Describe,
describe, describe.

On the other hand, if you are talking to a DFT, you should
focus on a few basic principles and conclusions. You want to provide clear options and clear reasons for preferring one option to
another. DFTs think in terms of choices. Once they pick up the
key points, they jump to the conclusions, and if you don't go
there with them, they will ignore everything else you say. They
are distracted and bored by details, by lengthy marshaling of
evidence, and by exploring every possible implication, unless
they are convinced first that this will help them see the choices

more clearly. They look for simplicity and respond well to bold, unqualified statements. They tend to accept or reject messages abruptly, so you need to grab them fast.

Finally, when you are talking with FTDs, you will do best if you frame your message in a larger context. You want to provide a clear story. FTDs want to see how things are connected and related. They object to black-and-white formulations, simplifications, and impersonality. They are more interested in connections than in conclusions and more interested in ripples than in methods. FTDs want to know who you are, because that is part of the context, and they want to interact with you, not simply listen. Try telling stories or anecdotes.

Life is not so conveniently arranged, however, that you will be able to tailor your messages so simply. You will often be unclear about the other person's pattern or you will be speaking with several people of differing patterns. Your best strategy then is to rely on your knowledge of yourself, your knowledge of how you are likely to be misread or how you are likely to provide a misleading display of your perceptions.

Strengthening your display

When you're interacting with another person, you are – among other things – displaying your perceptions for that person. And since your perceptions are valuable, you want to display them so they are not misread. You can use your knowledge of your TDF pattern to help you here. One way you will be misread is when you focus too narrowly on the language fitting your big perceptual lens, the first letter of your pattern. Another way you will be misread is when you neglect the language fitting your small lens, your last letter.

TDFs and TFDs typically focus on the T-language of content when they are communicating. They attend to their content and to their words. They use language with care, because they want to be clear and accurate. One danger this focus on T-language poses is that in trying to be precise, in trying to be accurate, they will obscure their message with excessive precision. Remember our example of a TDF order: do A, then B, then C, then D. At its best, this is brilliantly clear and useful. At its worst – think about IRS instructions – it tries to cover every possible case and every possible contingency and ends up muddying rather than clarifying. *Do A unless R and T are both true at time S, in which case do B, unless R is true and T is false, in which case do C.* This is not clarity. True clarity requires clear context and clear conclusions as well as clear content.

Narrow focus on T-language creates the fallacy that *the facts speak for themselves.* Erin is a TFD financial analyst who likes to present tables of information to her clients and let them draw their own conclusions. These tables of information seem so obvious to her that she feels silly pointing out the obvious. This is wrong. Facts never speak; facts require spokespeople and advocates who will give the facts context and conclusions. The belief that the conclusions and the connections are too obvious to require spelling out is always wrong. What is obvious to you is not obvious to others. The facts do not speak to everyone with the eloquence they have for TFDs and TDFs.

DFTs and DTFs typically focus on the D-language of conclusions. They prefer simple messages, starting with the conclusion and attending sharply to the options present in this situation. They dislike elaborating, citing evidence, piling up examples, or dealing with remote consequences. They see these things as redundant, irrelevant, and confusing. *Enough said, let's go.* They see choices as simple and black-and-white, and have trouble understanding that elaboration might help others. A DFT giving directions to a restaurant may just wave her hand and say, "It's over that way." Nothing could be simpler. In fact, this may be much too simple. The great D-language fallacy is that *conclusions and actions speak for themselves.* Directions often require street names and distances. Conclusions often require both the evidence of content and the elaboration of context. We know a CEO who once flew across the country to interview candidates for sales manager in a very small branch operation. He was sending a powerful message about the importance of branch sales and his unhappiness with branch sales, but he never explicitly said this. He thought his actions were statement enough. His actions were certainly noticed − CEO's are always noticed − but the range of interpretations of his actions was astounding. His message was poorly read because he didn't explain his actions.

FTDs and FDTs typically focus on the F-language of context. They pack their messages with connections. We have a friend who jokes that she always knows when an FTD has left her a voice mail, because the message is always seven minutes long. There is always some risk that an FTD or FDT, in his effort to help you see the picture, will start at the creation of the world to explain why he is calling you and why you should call back. If you are an FTD or an FDT, you may provide too much context with too much complexity. Try to get to your point more quickly and make sure that you have a point you are getting to. This will feel clumsy and abrupt, but your audiences will love you. The great F-language fallacy is the belief that the connections speak for themselves, that if you tell a good enough story, you do not need to point out why you are telling the story. You don't need to give the story a moral, because the moral is obvious. Again, however, what is obvious to you is not obvious to all.

FDTs and DFTs, on the other hand, often ignore the need for precision and simple clarity is lost in the mix. One of us − a small-T − used to make writing assignments when he was teaching, and when the students would ask for some instructions about what the paper should look like, he would respond, with a wave of the hand, "Whatever you want, just make it interesting." This was not helpful. The students wanted to know how long the paper should be, how many references they should use, whether spelling and grammar would count, and similar factual concerns, and their desire to know these things was perfectly correct. Mind reading should not be a course requirement.

TFDs and FTDs have trouble simplifying. All the facts, all the steps, all the connections seem equally important and the thought of dropping some facts and connections seems to gut the entire discussion. This makes them sound evasive and lost in detail. Their directions to the restaurant may be so elaborate that you can't remember them, and so you get lost.

TDFs and DTFs underplay the value of context. A DTF's voice mail message, for example, might be: "This is Mike. Call me." Mike neglects to mention *why* you should call him. Mike should try to include more context, more reasons why, and also try to elaborate his message a bit. He should ask himself, why should these people care about what I am saying?

To see ourselves as others see us

We're making a simple claim here. We're suggesting that you will do better in your journeys if you take responsibility for understanding others and responsibility for helping them understand you. Living and working well with others is not a matter of tricks and gimmicks. It is a matter of responsibility, maturity, and respect. We're often asked what patterns get along the best and what patterns clash the most. The quality of our relationships, however, does not center on pattern; it centers on responsibility and respect. You will do well with people of each of the six patterns if you take responsibility for understanding them and respect the ways in which they are different than you. Our differences can enrich our lives. It may be easier to get away with being irresponsible with people who are more similar to you, but that is not a formula for success.

Remember our friend Jack, the FTD manager with whom we began this chapter? Jack became a better FTD manager when he recognized that his greatest talents were often difficult for his employees and peers to see and that they often saw his vulnerabilities more than his strengths. His great talent is his sense of context and connection and his ability to win the commitment and loyalty of employees and customers. His vulnerability is his difficulty in rapidly seeing conclusions. His employees, however, were looking for his conclusions – what's he going to do with this department? – and were less interested in the connections he was building. He took responsibility for helping people see what he was doing, that he was building a department around commitment, loyalty, and a sense of shared connection, a sense that "we're in this together." Jack didn't have to become a DTF to succeed; he only had to become a more responsible FTD.

14

Finding Your Place

Knowing yourself should help you choose more wisely the vocational, community, and spiritual settings that fit you best. We each thrive best in different settings, the settings that reward our strengths and do not attack our weaknesses.

"Know yourself" is advice hallowed by its antiquity. The Greek oracle at Delphi offered this counsel 2500 years ago, and at about the same time both Lao Tze and Confucius put this guidance at the heart of the Asian wisdom traditions. Down the centuries this advice has echoed, and someone probably said it last week on Oprah's show. So what's the big deal? Knowing yourself seems simple enough. You hear your thoughts, you know your secrets, and you see yourself in action every conscious moment. You know your dreams, your hopes, and your fears. You have seen yourself succeed and you have seen yourself fail. You would seem to know yourself more intimately and more accurately than you could ever know any other person, so why are these sages acting as if this is both a great mystery and a great prize?

"Know yourself" is good counsel because knowing yourself allows you to choose more wisely. If you know yourself, you know what you can do skillfully and what you cannot. You know what you enjoy and what you do not. You know when you can be helpful and when you will be welcome. You know what relationships might be possible and rewarding and what relationships might be difficult and punishing. You know when you are reading a situation well and when you are indulging in wishful thinking. You know what to expect of yourself. In a word, when you know yourself, your choices will be well founded, set in reality rather than illusion, framed by possibilities rather than impossibilities.

We know this advice is difficult, however, simply because we make so many bad choices. We don't mean choices that happen to turn out badly. Since both our knowledge and our power are limited, we have limited control over how events will unfold. Good choices can have bad results. Chance is a real factor in our lives and risk is a constant presence in our choices. Our bad choices are those that could only have bad results: we accept the wrong jobs; we love the wrong people; we accept responsibilities we cannot meet; and we ignore responsibilities that we must meet. The predictable results are that we fail, we are hurt, we are overburdened, and we suffer the consequences of our ignorance. We look back later and say, "I should have known better." And we should know better. We should be wiser.

Choosing wisely rests on realism. We cannot choose well if we don't know the territory. Packing jungle gear for a trip to Alaska would be a poor choice. The consequences would be uncomfortable at best. We need to know something about the world in which we travel, and we need to know something about ourselves. Am I the kind of person who loves the jungle or am I the kind of person who loves the Arctic? We need maps and guides to avoid the wrong turns.

We've offered you a map and a guide to yourself – the TDF map. The test of this map, like any map, is in your travels. Can our map help guide you? Can our map help you make better choices? The quality of our choices is the mark of our wisdom. How can we make better choices?

A few years ago, we worked with Janet, a bank executive who was financially successful but unhappy and thinking of a career change. About halfway through a workshop, she approached us and said, "I'd been thinking about becoming a preschool teacher, but I'm a DTF, so I guess that won't work." We were appalled. She was stereotyping preschool teaching as work that she, as a DTF, could not do. We're not here to forbid you to act on your dreams. We simply want you to make your choices and realize your dreams within a framework of realism and self-understanding. We want you to know yourself so you know the difference between a dream and an illusion. A dream is possible; an illusion is not. Our dreams shape our successes; our illusions shape our failures.

Sorting our dreams and possibilities from our fantasies and illusions is a key wisdom. Were Janet's musings about becoming a teacher realistic dreams or illusory fantasies? If her fantasy was more about "becoming an FTD" than about becoming a teacher, then Janet was playing with illusions. The idea that you can become a different kind of person – tempting though it sometimes is – is always an illusion. Sometimes we believe that because we are unhappy, we need to become somebody else, somebody very different than we are. We become tired of our struggles and envy those who don't seem to share those struggles. We forget that everyone faces problems. We imagine that other lives are simpler and happier than ours are. This is a terrible – and terribly common – mistake. Our unique perspective on ourselves misleads us. I know that I am frightened or bored or sad, but I don't see your doubts and misgivings. You look competent, cool, and content. So perhaps I should try to become like you.

"Pattern jumping" can never be the answer. You cannot escape yourself. You cannot run from your talents and responsibilities. If Janet thought we were saying she could not become an FTD, she was right. Janet cannot travel that path. But if Janet thought becoming an FTD would improve her life, she was wrong. She had no need to escape her pattern, because there is nothing wrong with her pattern. There is nothing wrong with any of the six patterns. Your pattern is not the source of any of your problems or unhappiness, although not understanding or accepting your pattern may well be a source of pain for you. Janet was not unhappy because she is a DTF, and she would certainly not find happiness by pretending to be an FTD. Of course Janet can be a preschool teacher, but she would have to be a DTF preschool teacher. Was that what she wanted?

Janet needed to look at what her unhappiness was telling her. Perhaps her unhappiness was the transient "I-need-a-vacation-or-somebody's-going-to-get-hurt" unhappiness we all feel from time to time, and the thought of becoming a preschool teacher was no different than fantasizing about Waikiki or the Virgin Islands (which must certainly amuse preschool teachers). Janet was sure, however, that a vacation would not help. "I would never come back," she said. This suggests that she was in the wrong place, that she was not in a place that makes the best use of her talents.

We began this book by talking about our "placement theory of happiness," and now we are back where we started. You do well if you are in settings that encourage you to make use of your strengths and give you some shielding from your limitations. You do poorly if you are in settings that make demands on your limitations and don't challenge your strengths. Your healthy settings will challenge you, but your unhealthy settings will stress you. Janet was stressed, not challenged, and this stress was chronic. Chronic stress and burnout suggest that you are in the wrong place.

No job is perfect. The image of a job as a source of endless happiness is itself an illusion. Endless happiness is not a good test for choosing your right settings. No job could pass this test; no relationship could pass this test. We've never known anyone who wasn't sporadically frustrated, bored, irritated, or weary of the work she does. Nor should we expect to draw all of our satisfactions from a job. We also need family, friends, communities, and artistic and spiritual engagements, and your best answer to your unhappiness may be to make changes in other areas of your life. Janet should consider whether she is seeking satisfactions from her work that work cannot give. A job cannot replace friends, family, love, and spiritual growth. But if you are consistently bored by your job, then that job isn't challenging you and engaging your strengths. If you are consistently drained, stressed, and burnt-out, then your job is challenging your limits, not your strengths. This is what Janet was experiencing. She felt good about other areas of her life. Work was her issue.

We need to take responsibility for our unhappiness. If you are unhappy in your job – or in your marriage or in your friendships or in your spiritual life – you need to take responsibility for your choices. Perhaps you are not making good use of your strengths in this setting. Perhaps you have been trying to succeed in this setting by someone else's rules and expectations. Perhaps you have mastered the challenges that first drew you into this setting and you need new challenges. We suggested this to Janet. Perhaps she could find new ways to use her strengths and thrive in her job. Use your imagination. You don't have to do things as you always have, and you don't have to do things as others taught you. How can you do your job differently, how can you do your relationships differently, so that your strengths are better challenged and your limits better protected?

If you find that you cannot act differently so that this setting works for you, you still have choices. If you cannot thrive in this setting, then consider moving on. There are many settings where you cannot thrive. There are, however, others in which you can. The price of being in the wrong setting is too high.

People often say to us, "I can't risk change because I have responsibilities I must meet." We certainly want you to act responsibly, but we don't want you to hide behind your responsibilities. If Janet decided to shift from banking to teaching, her income would drop dramatically. This would affect her family and this is a realistic consideration. Many people, however, have found that their paths do not require a large income and that other rewards are more important to them. Finding your place will certainly require that you pay some costs. Many artists have worked dull, menial jobs in the day so they can create at night. Many lawyers who love trial work loathed law school. No one said life is idyllic or easy. There is a wonderful Spanish proverb, "Take whatever you like, says God, but pay for it." Find your place and pay for it. You will certainly pay much more if you do not find your place. Settling for less than you could be is a high price to pay.

We suggested that Janet look at her unhappiness more carefully. Had she always been unhappy in her work in banking? If not, what had changed? What's different now and what did this tell her? When had she felt good about her work and what did this tell her? Was she being asked to do work that drained her, work that drew heavily on her limits and vulnerabilities? Was her work providing opportunities to draw on her talents?

In the end, Janet decided that preschools were simply an escapist fantasy for her. She was unhappy because recent corporate changes had left her feeling unappreciated and dead-ended. A merger had transformed the management landscape, and the new environment felt too "political" for her. She was unsure whom she could trust and depend upon, and this uncertainty was draining her. As a DTF, the politics, the jockeying, the probing of loyalties felt like quicksand to her. What she really wanted was the world she had before the merger, but because she knew that was impossible, she began to fantasize about escaping to a completely new world. Banking still fit her, but her current bank no longer did. She needed to move, but she didn't need a completely new world. Three months later she had found a new job, through a former colleague who had also left the bank. She checked carefully the political environment of her new bank before moving and found an environment where she felt more comfortable. There are no guarantees about the future, of course, but when we last checked, she felt she had made a very good choice.

But what if Janet had decided to leave banking? Would preschool teaching have been a good choice? We would have asked Janet to reflect on her experience and her sense of her talents and her limits. Then we would have asked her to use her imagination to build a detailed picture of what her life would be like as a preschool teacher. We'd suggest that she visit preschools to enrich her picture and that she talk with people who work in preschools. Imagining skillfully requires knowledge and information or it is simply daydreaming and escaping. Could Janet truly picture herself thriving in this setting? Janet would need a clear picture of herself, as well as a clear picture of the world of preschools. She is a DTF. She is nourished by settings that call for strength and focus; she is drained by settings that call for patiently cultivating networks of relationships and nurturing harmonious connections. Could she see how she could use her talents in this new setting? Could she see how Janet fits?

How do we make good choices? We choose using our experience, our imagination, and our images of our worlds and ourselves. So we choose better when we reflect upon our experiences and learn our lessons. We choose better when we enrich our sense of reality and possibility with a disciplined imagination. We choose better when we find, test, and use the best guides and maps of our worlds and our lives. We've sung this song throughout this book. We've stressed these tools – experience, imagination, and maps – because they are the tested tools of humanity, the tools on which all our traditions rest.

Your experience gives you a wealth of information: where have you succeeded and where have you failed? What tasks have engaged you and what tasks have frustrated you? Where have you felt nourished and where have you felt drained? Think of your life as a series of experiments. What have you learned from the results? These are not casual questions to be answered on the fly. These questions demand thought and reflection, but we hope that in reading this book, you have been thinking and reflecting as you've experimented with the images and maps we've laid out for you. Experience is useless until you reflect upon it and learn from it.

Your imagination is another great tool. Imagining is often belittled in the name of a "hard-boiled realism," but true realism requires imagination. Reality is not simply what is in front of you at this moment. Reality is much larger. Reality includes possibilities, connections, contexts, and facts that are not immediately present. The "hardboiled realism" that disparages imagination presents a small and impoverished world, a world without dreams and possibilities. This is not reality; this is mediocrity. Imagining is the great gift that takes us beyond what is immediately present. Imagining does require discipline and testing to distinguish possibility from impossibility, but without imagining, we lose our sense of possibility.

Finally, you need maps and guides. Your journey is unique, but you are not the first person to journey. Others have learned things that can help you, just as what you learn can help others. Knowing whether a choice can work for you requires that you know something of your world and of yourself. Who you are creates your possibilities. That's what a good map of yourself gives you: a sense of the possibilities. Knowing who you are should help you see which choices are good and which are not. We hope TDF is giving you a better sense of yourself, of your strengths, your talents, your potential, and your limits. We hope we are giving you a better map of the territory of your life, and we hope that you use our map as well as other maps and guides. Having a map, however, is not the same thing as making the journey. The journey is yours to make.

Seeing the best path isn't easy. We sometimes get lost. We sometimes find ourselves in settings that are too difficult, where we will fail. We sometimes find ourselves in settings that we have outgrown and need to leave. We hope TDF is helping you understand that when you fail or flounder, this does not mean you are defective. You are in the wrong place. Have the courage to find your own path. Henry David Thoreau, reflecting on the life he created for himself at Walden Pond, said:

I learned this, at least, by my experiment; that if one advances confidently in the direction of his dreams, and endeavors to live the life which he has imagined, he will meet with a success un-expected in common hours.

Thoreau is suggesting that the courage and the imagination to be yourself are the great resources for your journey. We would only add that a sense of who you are, a map of yourself, can support your courage and shape your imagination. Knowing the kind of person you are, knowing the kind of journey you are on, is the beginning of wisdom. This is why the sages of our traditions have urged us to this knowledge. Knowing the kind of person you are can guide you. Knowing that every path is not your path can save you from needless frustration and pain. Knowing who you are gives you a firm compass in these turbulent times. You don't have to be anyone but yourself.

And others have to be themselves. There is much we can do for each other in our journeys. We can help each other; we can rely on each other; we can support each other; we can care about each other. What we cannot do is choose for each other. My choices are mine and yours are yours. We can learn, however, to honor each other's choices and honor our differences. This is true respect.

The most important feature of the TDF map is our insistence that our differences are good. You don't have to be somebody you are not. If we have succeeded with this book, you should have a greater sense of your strengths and your possibilities. You don't need to be anyone else. You don't need to be who you are not. You don't have to be "fixed." You simply have to be yourself.

Our differences are real. These differences are the key to the map we have offered you. A DFT will have hopes and fears that differ from a TFD, because a DFT has different strengths and limits, different challenges and vulnerabilities. A DFT sees a different world that does the TFD, so a DFT walks a different path. Only when we are able to see our differences, only when we make our differences part of our maps, can we also honestly see what unites us, our common humanity. Knowing yourself means knowing that other people are different than you and not expecting them to act as you would act or to react as you would react. That is realism. Knowing yourself means knowing that there are paths you should not walk, paths that are meant for others but not for you. That is realism. Most importantly, knowing yourself means knowing your possibilities, knowing the paths you can walk. Knowing your possibilities is your greatest realism.